THE INIMITABLE HENRY KISSINGER

"It took me years to be thoroughly loathed at Harvard. Here in Washington it happened almost overnight."— Henry Kissinger once said with a touch of sadness behind the sarcasm.

"He was secretive. He sat in that overstuffed chair studying from morning until night and biting his nails, till there was blood."—*A Harvard schoolmate*

"He walked around expecting everyone to notice him because he was extraordinary—a fat lump of 'extraordinariness' with that awful accent."—*A former classmate.*

"Maybe it can't be done, but if anybody can do it, Kissinger can."—*Joe Sico, Ass't Secretary of State for Near Eastern and South Asian Affairs.*

In Nancy Kissinger's view, Henry is a warm, almost ebullient man with an enormous interest in other people. She finds that he talks with an animated curiosity to foreign ministers and gardeners alike. "Whatever you say to him, he finds it important."

"Henry praises only estimates of strength and force. If you do not have a nuclear bomb under your pillow, he is not interested."—*Danielle Hunebelle, French writer.*

KISSINGER:
HIS RISE AND ?

DAVID HANNA

MANOR
BOOKS
INC.

A MANOR BOOK 1975

Manor Books Inc.
432 Park Avenue South
New York, New York 10016

KISSINGER:
HIS RISE AND ?

PART ONE

What Makes Henry Run

Bismarck, Henry Kissinger wrote, was a man of many roles and many seasons. "What is an opportunist?" he once was asked. "He is a man who uses the most favorable opportunity to carry through what he regards as useful and appropriate."

CHAPTER 1

What Jane Russell did for Cup D., Jackie Kennedy for Long Island *chic*, Ethel Kennedy for mini-skirts, Eisenhower for golf and Senator Sam Ervin for Shakespeare and the Bible, Secretary of State Henry Kissinger accomplished for political crying.

When the good Henry stepped before the TV cameras in Salzburg in the spring of 1974 and told a press conference that he intended resigning unless the Senate Foreign Relations Committee gave his integrity a vote of confidence, tears welled into his dark-brown eyes and the familiar horn-rims couldn't conceal them. They weren't cheek-splashing tears but, no doubt about it, they were the genuine article, *bona fide lacrimae*.

Kissinger, it turned out, had been brooding about a new inquiry by the Committee into his role in the wiretapping of thirteen Government officials and four newsmen in 1969-1970. They had been digging into charges that Kissinger, then

President Nixon's chief advisor on foreign affairs and architect of his administration's global policies, was far more involved in initiating and following up on the wiretaps than he had admitted and that Kissinger had lied in telling the Committee in the fall of 1973 that he merely supplied some names of his staff to the White House snoopers on the President's orders.

Kissinger wailed that he had told the Senators the truth and that any stain on his moral fiber would render him incapable of functioning in the high level, confidential negotiations required of a Secretary of State. Reporters, surprised at the diplomat's unexpected outburst and uncharacteristic loss of poise, wondered at their significance, particularly since they occurred en route to Richard Nixon's triumphal tour of the Middle East where Kissinger, several weeks earlier, had achieved the diplomatic miracle of a shaky peace. There had to be deeper implications and consider too where the threat took place! Right at the frontier of the land of *The Third Man!*

That evening coffee houses and *Weinstuben* buzzed with rumors and whispers. As visiting correspondents hung up their trench coats and joined them, smug smiles lighted up the faces of the local Austrian journalists who looked knowingly out the windows, aware they possessed the secret to Kissinger's temper tantrum. "It is *der Foehn.* That's what started it. It had to be. Doesn't it always happen in Salzburg?"

Der Foehn, they explained, is the catch-all scapegoat for everything that goes wrong in that scenic paradise, the Austrian Alps. It is a wind peculiar to the region which blows across the plateau of South Europe from Turkey, a steady, monotonous air current whose persistence affects the nerves. *Der Foehn* is blamed for a wide variety of ailments, from pulmonary disorders to ingrown toenails—and mental depression. Especially the last. *Der Foehn* has been known to drive star-crossed lovers to suicide, international financiers to abandoning their mistresses and Austria's spy colony to come out of the cold and flee to the lush tropical vegetation of Rio. And now it had grasped Henry Kissinger in its sinister currents!

"Not to worry," the Austrians reassured their colleagues, as they ordered another bottle of wine and asked the zither player for *Vienna, City of My Dreams*, for the twenty-ninth time, "It will all blow over—if you will forgive the pun."

Back in the United States deceased Secretaries of State, Thomas Jefferson, Daniel Webster, George C. Marshall and certainly John Foster Dulles, spun in their graves. J. William Fulbright, Chairman of the Foreign Relations Committee, cloaked his frosty visage in the warmest of expressions, the slightest hint of a smile at the edge of his thin lips as he commented that Kissinger had been overworking and "he probably needs a good night's sleep."

As far as the American people were concerned, the sight of a tear-stained Henry Kissinger was all right with them. He had *Kissingerized* them again. The average Joe had no idea of what Henry *really* did—but at least they could see the results of his handiwork, the shaky end of the Vietnam war, the shaky peace in the Middle-East, shaky *detente* with the Soviet Union. "So let the kraut cry a little," they said over their beer in neighborhood bars. "He's entitled to it."

Kissinger had gotten away with something few politicians have weathered—breaking down in public. Edmund Muskie cried his chances for the Democratic Presidential nomination away on the day he stood in front of the offices of William Loeb, publisher of the *Union*, in Manchester, New Hampshire, and wept over Loeb's scurrilous personal remarks about his wife. Tom Eagleton was given short shrift by the public when his eyes filled and his face perspired as he bowed out of the Democratic vice-presidential nomination. "Look at him," the bar crowds murmured, "just like they say. He's some kind of nut."

So it remained for Henry Kissinger to break the old rule that thoroughbreds—and politicians—don't cry. He had made ping-pong a household word, popularized horn rims, established the tenacity of sex in Nixon's asexual White House and now Kissinger could claim credit for having endowed political tears with respectability.

His Salzburg adventure was the first of a torrent that poured from political eyes in the last months of the Nixon administration. Press Secretary Ronald Ziegler specialized in wet eyes and the tight lip. Senator Robert Griffin, second ranking Republican in Congress featured the cracking voice, clenched fist, groping-for-words technique when he told TV audiences that, indeed, Richard Nixon had masterminded the Watergate cover-up. Chairman Peter Rodino, of all people, fought back tears when he pounded the gavel for the last time on the House Impeachment Hearings—and he couldn't have been devoted that much to the job. "He's trying on tears for the campaign" quipped one D.C. tear statistician.

For the record, Pennsylvania's Hugh Scott didn't cry—to anyone's knowledge, not did Senators Eagleton or Muskie. The Nixons had the courtesy to do most of their crying in private—the President, Plastic Patricia, the daughters, the Eisenhower grandson and the Cox boy. But the discipline broke down at the conclusion of Richard Nixon's resignation speech when a bombshell exploded on television. Nixon closed with moist eyes and the camera panned in on moist-eyed CBS correspondent Dan Rather who pronounced the event "majestic." It was as though Rather had suddenly given up his Eagle Scout badge as Nixon's most vocal and sarcastic critic in the TV press gallery. Roger Mudd looked on in horror as he quickly took over and assaulted the self-serving resignation speech as a final remorseless example of Tricky Dick's political morality.

When Richard Nixon and Gerald Ford swapped jobs the following morning the two residents might as well have officiated at the opening of National Crying-jag Week. On the White House lawn Nixon rambled on for nineteen tearful moments about his mother whom he described as a "saint" and his old man who had never amounted to much in the eyes of the world but who was a great person nonetheless.

Finally, after taking the oath of office, President Gerald Ford addressed the American people, his voice broke and his eyes moistened with the words, "May our former President who brought peace to millions find it for himself."

The driest eyes at the ceremonies on that balmy August morning belonged to the bland, expressionless face of Secretary of State Henry Kissinger, whose honor had meantime been affirmed by the Senate and whose continuance as top man at Foggy Bottom had been personally requested by Gerald Ford and announced even before he was sworn in.

The rumpled refugee from Nazi Germany, looking more like an owlish pixie than the Dr. Strangelove so beloved of caricaturists, had come a long way, baby, and no one knew it better than he.

Things were damp enough around the White House without Dr. Kissinger throwing in his two tears' worth. Moreover, he had just accomplished one of the most difficult jobs of his life as the key man in a triumvirate involved in patiently moving an immovable object from one position to another. The immovable force was President Richard Nixon whom they had pink-slipped.

The others were James St. Clair, Nixon's own attorney, who blew his stack, when former Ensign Dick riffled through an old gunnysack and came up with a dusty tape recording of a conversation with White House aides, clearly implicating him in keeping the lid on the Watergate caper. The other was White House Chief of Staff Alexander Haig.

When Haig learned of the tape and Nixon's plan to make it public, prodded by attorney St.

Clair, he realized the Nixon Presidency had collapsed and the first order of business was to get to Kissinger.

Haig slipped out of the White House by one of the side doors used so often in the Nixon years that the front door hinges rusted. He eluded newspapermen's *death watch* and hurried through the humid streets of the capital to the State Department and into Kissinger's office where the worried expression on Haig's face told the Secretary of State all he needed to know.

For months the old friends had been standing in the wings, looking for the guillotine to fall, expecting the moment when their duty would force them to renounce their loyalty to Richard Nixon and step out onto the world stage and into history as the men who shepherded the president into his escape hatch.

It was nasty business. Haig and Kissinger both owed Nixon deep personal and career debts. He was, in cold reality, the man who had made them both, the source of their power. Now they were about to use that power to unmake the most powerful authority in the world, a leader elected by forty-seven million people who had become hopelessly entrapped in the two-year tangle of his own deceit, forced into a confession of past lies, deserted by his most faithful defenders. Neither General Haig's Army or Henry Kissinger's State Department carried position papers on how to dispose of a Chief Executive.

It wasn't going to be easy. They were dealing with a volatile, deeply disturbed individual who they knew had already considered stonewalling some more as the last line of defense. Old-fashioned methods, like hemlock and exile to the desert, were discarded out of hand and snooping on Democrats certainly wasn't worth the price of a pearl-handle revolver. And those diamonds for Plastic Patricia didn't rate a firing squad. They decided on resignation, the modish way so common to Madison Avenue which, after all, had manufactured the President's images, the new Nixon in 1968 and the new, new Nixon in 1972.

Americans aren't the dopes the polls and political leaders assume them to be. They'd been watching Nixon under the microscope of TV and their eyes told them what the liberal press, the Eastern establishment and the elitests politely overlooked, that the man who fumbled for words in the Oval office of the White House, who sweat like a wrestler, whose hand trembled and whose mind clearly wandered was not a cunning Tricky Dick of old.

Something had gone astray—maybe Patricia's cooking. Maybe Golda Meir should have sent him some chicken soup along with her thanks. Maybe he was reacting to the awful burden of the tall tales he kept repeating to the American people—and chicken soup has never cured deception.

Realizing this, Kissinger and Haig quickly urged Secretary of Defense James Schlesinger to keep his eye on that little black bag with all the buttons. Secretary of the Treasury William Simon was instructed to button up the cabinet, warning that the slightest false note in the orchestration might freeze Nixon into a position of continuing his lonely struggle to escape removal from office. Only two nights earlier, aboard the Potomac, Nixon had played the role of the *Defiant One*— the gut fighter who intended rolling back the avalanche of revulsion at his shabby White House conduct. The man literally believed that some magical formula would materialize to vindicate him and carry him forward to greater and greater triumphs.

No one was kidding anybody in the hours of those *Five Days of August* when they described the United States as a *Banana Republic*.

Distinguished Congressional leaders were summoned to the White House and blandly told reporters afterward that the visit amounted to nothing more than a frank appraisal of the situation in the House and Senate where Nixon's support had dwindled away to virtually nothing. No, no, a thousand times no, they had not mentioned the nasty word "resignation."

Kissinger and Haig had orchestrated well. Barry Goldwater and Hugh Scott looked embarrassed. They knew they were fooling no one, that they were mere notes in a symphony, waiting for the conductor to tell them when to play.

Henry Kissinger, the fellow out of nowhere, the intellectual, the rumpled Harvard professor who had stumbled into Washington in the Eisenhower and Kennedy days as an unknown quantity, mildly sinister, suspiciously European, yet curiously if briefly at home in the pseudo-elegance of the Kennedy atmosphere, became the man closest to the embattled President.

Did he expect it? How prepared was he? What were his private thoughts? Kissinger will one day have an enormously fascinating story to tell history. Sadly, like too many things about the Nixon years, historians will never be able to test its accuracy—regardless of Kissinger's protestations. The Nixon men for too long distorted a once uncluttered English word "credibility."

Kissinger, St. Clair and Haig were walking on eggs during that last week of Nixon grandstanding. They responded to his questions by implication rather than direct answers. They sought to clarify the facts of his deteriorated political position to Nixon's cloudy mind, but avoided giving the reasons. They were silent when Nixon, looking at them beseechingly, mused, "I campaigned for a lot of people. Some were turkeys, but I campaigned for all of them. Where are they now?"

There wasn't much sense in trying to answer Nixon's questions. Nixon—not the candidates he worked for—had destroyed his presidency. The men, guiding him toward the Oval Room statement of his resignation, were tragically aware they were dealing with a highly charged manic-depressive. All the indications of his volatile mental condition had been present since the first glimmer of his involvement in the Watergate break-in came to light via the *Washington Post.*

Alternately walking on a pink cloud of hope and excitement as some of Henry Kissinger's diplomatic missions bore fruit Nixon plunged almost instantaneously into a deep pit of despair as the worst political scandal in American history unfolded. In the final days of ruin the president's family could not be counted upon for rational decisions either. They completely cut themselves off from reality, huddling protectively around Richard Nixon, urging him to continue his fight against impeachment as he had promised—down to the point where he would accept with satisfaction the vote of a single senator.

In another situation a pragmatic man like Kissinger would have taken Julie Eisenhower aside and told her as diplomatically as possible to "get lost." She was the most militant and strident of the Nixon clan, dogging her father until the bitter end not to be a quitter. If it amounted to an admirable expression of a daughter's loyalty to her father, the shrill oppressiveness of her arguments reflected the young woman's political naivete, so often reflected when she took over the podium as spokeswoman for the Nixon interests.

That Julie Eisenhower was not scratched more deeply by the Washington press corps during her adolescent harangues in the Rose Garden and at carefully orchestrated public events was certainly no reflection on their capacities but the customary restraints imposed in dealing with someone woefully ill-equipped for her job. Mrs. Eisenhower would have profited from exposure to Margaret Truman, a young lady who finessed the Washington press corps with skill, charm and grace.

But the Nixon women wouldn't get lost—and no one expected them to, especially Henry Kissinger, the first of the triumvirate to understand that the President was conceding defeat. In a telephone call early in the week Nixon asked Kissinger what would happen to the world and to the country if he stayed in office or if he went. He was a man looking for support, knowing there was none, and the best he could expect was opinion. In the confusion surrounding Nixon's last week in the presidency White House logs became hopelessly tangled. There is no record of how many times he talked to Kissinger by phone and face to face.

But much has leaked out about those conversations. They appear to have been rehearsals for the embarrassing farewell to the White House staff in the East Room on the morning he quit office and flew to San Clemente.

Kissinger listened patiently as Nixon rambled, talking about everything but his immediate dilemma. While the world worried about the awesome consequences of his decision, Nixon prattled on about his boyhood, his Quakerism and the peace he so deeply believed in. He talked about prayer and affirmed his belief in the hereafter. He wanted to know if his place in history would be that of a man who had tried his best to bring peace to the world. Kissinger assured him it would. It was like dealing with a small child with a bellyache.

To veteran reporters much of the Nixon meanderings recalled the night he slid out of the White House at the height of the student demonstrations and walked over to the Lincoln Memorial where he found a group of kids and talked to them. "About football," one of them told reporters. "It was crazy, man. He looked so old and tired. All beat up. He never completed a sentence, just went on and on about football. Like some kind of nut.''

Wednesday turned out to be the moment of truth. Nixon and his family dined together—and cried. Kissinger was invited to the White House afterward. Kissinger stayed until well past midnight. Somewhere in the disjointed conversation Nixon told his Secretary of State that he intended resigning the following day. There didn't seem much more to be said after that meeting—but one more telephone call came shortly after Kissinger arrived home. They talked until one and that, to all appearances, was their last conversation until after the resignation speech.

Henry Kissinger had another president to consider, Gerald Ford.

On Thursday morning, Ford was at Blair House presenting Medals of Honor to the families of seven soldiers who had been killed in Viet Nam. By now the country was flooded with rumors that Nixon intended resigning. The ceremony was barely over when Ford was summoned to the Oval Office where Nixon told him of his decision to quit. It was immediately after that meeting that Kissinger felt assured that some of the syrupy talk he'd been dishing out to Richard Nixon in the last fortnight had a basis in fact. The Nixon foreign policy would be continued.

Ford's first telephone call on leaving Nixon was to Henry Kissinger. "I would like to talk to you some time this afternoon," he said. "I want to talk to you about staying on. So think about that." Kissinger reassured the Vice-President, "There will be no problem."

They met for two hours and since it occurred in the pre-pardon era of the Ford administration the conference was described as candid, characteristically "simple and direct."

Ford told Kissinger, "I need you," pointing out that they had known each other for years and had gotten along well. The President-to-be stressed that he didn't expect any trouble. Master diplomat Kissinger replied with true European finesse, "It is my job to get along with you and not your job to get along with me."

The two agreed that the quicker Kissinger's continuance as Secretary of State was made known the better. The State Department was told to send messages to all nations, assuring them of the continuity of U.S. foreign policy. That night, after watching Nixon's resignation speech on television with his family at home, Ford went outside into the drizzle and talked to reporters and his neighbors. Conceding that he'd witnessed the "saddest incident of his life" he announced that Kissinger, whom he called a "very great man" would stay on as Secretary of State.

There was another meeting with Kissinger on Friday morning as Ford feverishly completed preparations for the swearing-in ceremonies. Kissinger was there in the East Room when Nixon made his extemporaneous farewell to the members of his own administration and probably wished he weren't. It must have been a grisly experience for everyone, especially Kissinger. On the other hand Henry had had plenty of experience with Nixon mawkishness and unpredictability. Years of circling the globe in advance of the President and warning foreign officials. "Here comes Nixon, don't laugh" ought to have prepared him for the embarrassment.

Obviously whatever tranquilizers Nixon had taken the night before to account for his dry-eyed restraint in reading his farewell address to the world had worn off. As Nixon's stream-of-consciousness outpouring of self-pity and self-torment meandered on, the people who had called him Mr. President for over five years began looking awkwardly at their feet.

Finally it was over—the longest nineteen minutes in their memory. Gerald Ford accompanied Nixon and his entourage to the *Spirit of '76*. The Jet lifted into the air, sped toward California and an era ended.

Henry Kissinger was the lone survivor of what Richard Nixon described in accepting the Republican nomination in Miami's cavernous Convention Hall in 1968 as an "impossible dream."

Whether Heinz Alfred Kissinger's life has been clouded by his childhood in Nazi Germany depends on which biographer you read, Kissinger's frame of mind at the time of a particular interview or the context of the article in which it has been mentioned.

Heinz was born in the Bavarian city of Fuerth, not too many kilometers from Munich where Adolf Hitler staged his beer hall *putsch* in 1923, the year Heinz was born. And close by lay Nuremberg where Hitler would excite crowds of his followers with his promises of *Deustchland ueber alles* and "tomorrow the whole world." It was definitely not the best time for a nice Jewish boy to be born, but the Kissingers of his parents' generation, like those of many before, knew only too tragically that there were seldom periods in European history when the stars smiled on the birth of Jews. Pogroms didn't rate as hard news in Bavaria, especially in Munich or Nuremberg, hard core seats of anti-Semitism.

As a matter of history, Fuerth owed its birth to Jewish persecutions of the Fourteenth Century when the City Fathers of Nuremberg, so joyously celebrated in Wagner's *Die Meistersingeren of Nuremberg*, forbade Jews to live within the city limits. So they packed up and founded communities outside the area. One of them was Fuerth.

The Jewish influence brought prosperity and a splendid intellectual climate to Fuerth that accounted in the Twentieth Century for families like the Kissingers, headed by an intellectual father; managed, maneuvered and held together by a practical do-it-herself mother. When such unions produced offspring they were preordained to special roles in the world, whether their geographical origin was Fuerth or Washington Heights in the Bronx where the Kissingers eventually ended up.

Heinz's father, Louis, was a teacher of Greek and Latin at a girls' school. His father had been a teacher and, in the tradition of Old World Judaism, his occupation had been handed down to his son, with it, the traditions of religion. Louis Kissinger chose to pay only lip service to the Old Law, although he celebrated *Rosh Hashanah* and *Yom Kippur* appropriately. His wife, Paula, whom he had married the year before Heinz was born, presided over a kosher kitchen because for one thing, that was the cuisine she knew; for another, she was a superb cook.

For the Jews who lived there in the first part of this century Fuerth was a wonderful town; what Boston was to the Irish, Milwaukee to Germans; San Francisco, to Italians. Their own institutions, synagogues, publishing houses, schools and libraries, were of the highest quality. There existed a well-endowed Jewish Orphanage, dating back to the Seventeenth Century and the famous *Alte-Schule*, the synagogue which was first dedicated in 1617 and had known a long line of famous rabbis from Samson ben Joseph to Hirsh Janow and Wolf Hamburg.

Jewish influence didn't stop at the doors of their profitable businesses, comfortable, well-furnished homes or their institutions. For centuries Fuerth Jews had carried strong political clout and knew how to use it. They had been factors to German princes. They had fought for the Bavarian Jews in the Nineteenth Century and were the leaders of the industrial revolution. They knew their way around City Hall and were justifiably smug and complacent.

They were typical Germanic Jews with strong patriotic ties to the *Vaterland*, accumulated over generations of peaceful coexistence with their Aryan brothers and sisters. They weren't *wanderers*, and the first flexing of Nazi muscles may not have been reassuring but hardly rated panic. Not even in 1933 when Hitler successfully toppled Von Papen and Von Hindenberg to become Germany's Chancellor and *Fuehrer*.

They were wrong and Heinz Kissinger, who was ten years old when Hitler, Goebbels and Goering took over Germany, was among the first to feel the impact. He was plump, with sensitive, friendly eyes who looked owlish behind horn-rimmed glasses, bright, precocious, not a bad soccer player, a favorite with teachers because he was bright. He wore nice clothes, lived in a comfortable home, enjoyed a warm relationship with his parents and his brother, Walter. They all sang *Deutschland Ueber Alles* with fervor on patriotic occasions and considered themselves comfortable middle-class citizens of a decent country that, like every other land in the world, was suffering the shocks imposed by Great Depression. Unemployment threatened Germany's shaky economy and the bread lines in America that appeared every week in the *Wochenschau* at the movies worried intellectuals like Louis Kissinger who knew his country's survival depended on America's. Times were tough, but they were universally tough. But the Kissingers surely never considered themselves an oppressed, underprivileged ethnic minority. That changed.

Being Jewish in Germany in 1933 was like living in a nightmare. The persecution that mushroomed so suddenly wasn't the simple cut-and-dried terror of medieval times when villages were burned to the ground, males lined up before firing squads and women raped. The Nazi pogrom was cleverly wrapped in legality, innuendo, suggestion, persuasion, quiet dismissal of Jewish employees in the office of *Herr Direktor*. The neighborhood butcher suddenly couldn't deliver any more—no help. Then he couldn't remember where he stacked the roast. On park benches there blossomed signs painted in yellow, *Jueden Verboten* (Forbidden to Jews). In the same yellow there appeared posters on the windows of department stores, *Jueden Unverwuenscht* (Jews not wanted).

Mail suddenly went astray when addressed to Jews—this within the extraordinarily efficient German Postal Service. When letters did arrive, there was no attempt to hide the fact that they'd been scanned by some interested *beobachter*. They were carefully and obviously resealed and stamped by the inspector who had read them.

Life was brutal for the "visible" Jew—the man who ran a business, a store or a service. His windows were smashed in the middle of the night by marauding bands of young Storm Troopers; his equipment wrecked, his merchandise ruined, produce destroyed. For a time doctors, scientists, bankers, lawyers, even teachers could keep going. They were the professionals, still needed until Hitler dug deeper into the destruction of the German moral fiber. As fair-skinned blacks used to do in America "they passed." It was a dangerous game and they knew it. But not every German Jew could pack up overnight and flee to America. It took the Kissingers six long years—an odyssey no less complicated and frustrating than the long, anxious months they spent in a country they no longer recognized.

It was the kids who didn't stand a chance. They were the ones who couldn't "pass"—no way. In Fuerth, for instance, the Jews were proud of their own schools which their children attended. Those who went to the fine state-operated *gymnasiums* could be identified because they also went to weekly Hebrew school.

A Jewish kid stood in front of his colleagues as naked as the day he was born, vulnerable and prey for the bullies. Maybe his father was an "honorary Aryan," his Jewish mother the mistress of an S.S. officer who protected her, his uncle, a scientist-genius whose Jewish blood was overlooked by the Nazis in the interests of the "national good." There were any number of survival devices for Jews in those first years—until they dwindled away. But they were of little use to Jewish youth.

Henry and Walter were requested to leave the *gymnasium.* It was all quite legal, written down with typical German thoroughness. When a rabbinical school was available to Jewish students they were to be transferred there. This was the law, part of the Nazi Jewish decrees.

This meant the end of Henry's playing on the soccer team and the finish of friendship with fellow students. Often parents played the decisive role in ending the friendships of their children with Jews. If not Jew-haters they were simply afraid. What would their neighbors say? Within a year Jewish children all over Germany had become totally isolated—much more so than their elders. Old men who fought side by side in World War I and who had played chess for years in the local *Weinstube* still welcomed their Jewish friends. They had little to lose. Women, however, belonged to the "visible" Jewish community.

They shopped, had to put up with the neighbors. They were more conscious of the deadly accusation—Jew-lover. So their relationships with Jewish friends became furtive, even clandestine. But friendships persisted—and survived.

Kissinger, when he became an international figure, was compelled by the very nature of his position to talk about his boyhood in Nazi Germany and try to explain what it meant to him. There has always been wonder what psychic path Henry Kissinger travelled from his Fuerth boyhood to his present eminence as Secretary of State. To what extent did the Nazi experience spur him on?

Kissinger always insists that he was not scarred by Hitler's persecution. Yet he and his brother were dismissed from school. He saw his father discharged from his teaching post in 1933. Twelve of their relatives joined the six millions Jews killed by the Nazis throughout Europe.

When there were the Nazi rallies, the pagan torch light parades in nearby Nuremberg, the Storm Troopers hopped trains and spilled into the streets of Fuerth to harass the Jewish population. The streets became a battleground. The violence of the Nazi hate brigades inspired German children to form their own gangs. They worked out their own hostility on Heinz, Walter, and their classmates at the rabbinical school.

Paula Kissinger, spry and alert in her seventies, remembers. "Our children weren't allowed to play with the others," she recalled. "They stayed shut up in the garden. The Hitler youth, which included almost all the children of Fuerth, sang in ranks on the street and paraded in uniform and Henry and his brother would watch them, unable to understand why they didn't have the right to do what the others did. The boys stayed close together for protection."

Kissinger has mentioned walking to the other side of the street to avoid the street gangs but he pointed out that his boyhood beatings in Germany were administered by "other boys not by uniformed men with clubs." The point is strong, but it should be added that the same boys who beat up on the Jews were active candidates for the Hitler Youth troops. You could see them everywhere—those who had qualified—bright and blond and shiny in their fresh khaki uniforms. The key to admission to the Hitler Youth was incredibly simple—parental consent and their willingness to fork out the hundred marks or so to buy the youth's uniform, the swastika arm bands, the miniature billy club and the other equipment that went into the making of *Der Fuehrer's* young legions. These and the weekly dues.

In his recollections of the Nazi years Kissinger has gone to great lengths to emphasize the disparity between the persecutions prior to 1938 and those that came after—when the Kissingers had become refugees in America. The Kissingers fled in August, 1938, just three months before the infamous *Crystal Night* of November ninth and tenth when Hitler Youth and storm troopers went on a wild rampage against Jewish property and Jewish lives all over Germany. That was the end of the German-Jewish version of "passing."

There was a *Schuleheim* in Starnberg, outside of Munich, where Nazi big shots housed the young people of their honorary Nazi wives and Jewish girl friends. Or the offspring of Jews with connections among men of good will who got their friends' boys and girls into it out of their own affection. Overnight the school was virtually emptied as the headmaster, responding to telegrams and phone calls, accomplished the miraculous job of evacuating them one by one to Switzerland, Holland, France and Scandinavia.

Fritz Kraemer, who has been called *The Man Who Discovered Kissinger* is less sanguine about the Nazi experience. He said, "What the Nazis did to these people is unspeakable. You can do damage to the soul of a man and never touch his body. For five years, the most formative years (10 to 15), Henry had to undergo this horror. And the real horror is the breakdown of the world. Imagine what it means when your father, who was your authority, the father you admired is suddenly transformed into a little mouse."

Carl Friedrich, a retired Harvard government professor and friend of Kissinger said, "None of us are very good at self analysis. As the Germans say, 'You can't jump over your own shadow'. I think Henry regretted the conflict the Nazis created between Jews and Germans. He did not want to carry the burden of this frightful heritage. And psychic suffering—you don't want to put that out before journalists."

But Kissinger tenaciously minimizes the impact of those years, "My life is Fuerth seems to have passed without leaving any lasting impressions. I can't remember any interesting or amusing moments. That part of my life is not a key to anything. I was not consciously unhappy. I was not acutely aware of what was going on. For children, these things are not that serious. It is fashionable now to explain everything psychoanalytically, but let me tell you the political persecutions of my childhood are not what control my life."

"Kissinger has to be kidding," said a veteran American newspaperman. "I went to Germany as a student at the age of fifteen and I can tell you the exact date I saw Hitler riding his bulletproof car through the streets and the weekends he came to Munich and stopped for tea at the *Regina Palast Hotel*. My attitudes have damned well been affected by life under the Nazis although I was in no way personally affected. I knew Jews my own age and Jews who were older, and at fifteen, I know that my heart bled for them. And there was nothing especially sensitive about me then—or now."

There are those who say Kissinger's attitude is either a "merciful loss of memory" or "escapist theory." At the same time they do not believe him. Jewish refugees maintain it is a pose, calculated to identify himself as a pragmatist, that any emotional approach to this area of his life might undermine his diplomatic skills.

"If what Kissinger says is true about his youth," they say, "He must have been an utter idiot. Or, to be charitable, "going through a boyish phase."

Whatever, he's not exactly an idiot now.

The Statue of Liberty stands gracefully in the center of New York Harbor, holding the torch of

Liberty high above her head in a dramatic gesture of welcome to the "poor, tired and oppressed" of the Emma Lazarus poem engraved on its base.

By the time the "poor and the tired" get to meet Miss Liberty face to face they have also learned the full meaning of the word "oppressed." Miss Liberty and Miss Lazarus notwithstanding, the United States Immigration Service takes a dim view of the "tired and the poor." They are welcomed only after having met stringent immigration requirements which would not be nearly so offensive if they were limited to financial responsibility. But our government, in its zeal to protect her people from foreign "naughty naughties," has evolved a code of standards that turns the Statue of Liberty into a monument to bigotry.

The color of one's skin has a lot to do with the privilege of entering the U.S.A. as a visitor or immigrant. Traditionally, this has been the ugly starting point for American discrimination. In this last century we've also gotten around to recognizing political threats to the corn crop like anarchists, Communists, socialists, free-thinkers, journalists who've written about them, Soviet birdwatchers and Czechoslovakian toy manufacturers. Unmarried adults who admit indulging in sexual intercourse are not welcome, and better to have a carrier of bubonic plague than a moral leper like a male homosexual or lesbian. And save us from anyone entering our shore who intends going into "peonage." Yep, that's one of the things Immigration wants to know—and asks the question with a straight face.

It was even tougher getting into the United

States in the Hitler years when our country's traditional open door policy toward political refugees had not penetrated the ranks of the consular officials processing visas. Thomas Mann and Albert Einstein, of course, met no trouble obtaining "honored resident alien status"—as well they should have. Both distinguished gentlemen may later have regretted taking advantage of it when their own loyalties to democratic *ideals* were question by the McCarthyites, but for the Hitler years they were both where they should have been, leading productive lives and making a sizeable contribution to their age.

However, for the rank and file German Jew emigrating to America was anything but easy. It required enormous patience on the part of the refugee battling red tape in Europe and the sponsoring parties involved in making the necessary guarantees in America. Nothing could throw Immigration into a tizzy quicker than sensing the possibility that an eighty-year old European grandmother with five sons in America, dividing thirty degrees among them, all married to career women whose collective income amounted to two-hundred thousand annually might become a public charge.

In 1938, President Roosevelt told Immigration to "Knock it off—that they were making our nit-picking policies the laughing stock of the civilized world." This was the year in which Hitler destroyed every synagogue in Germany, put thirty-five thousand Jews into concentration camps and appropriated all Jewish personal and business property over two thousand dollars. Immigration relaxed the stiff requirements.

Paula Kissinger spearheaded the exodus of her family. Paula had an aunt in London who helped them get to England where it was less difficult to obtain refugee status and take what for the Kissingers was to become the most important step of their lives—migrating to America.

The senior Kissingers with Henry and Walter were part of the 1938 wave of German refugees who had come to America in such numbers, settling in Washington Heights at the northern tip of Manhattan, that the section became known as the *Fourth Reich*. It was already heavily populated with Jews, refugees of other persecutions, mostly those who had fled the pogroms of czarist Russia. They were the older residents; their totally Americanized children and grandchildren had little in common with the new arrivals beyond sympathy. There was not even the bond of language, since few of the German refugees spoke Yiddish.

Becoming Americanized wasn't going to be easy, but the Kissingers, especially Paula and Heinz, were strong and resilient. It wasn't simple to adjust to poverty for the first time in their lives, acute, daily poverty, for the business of earning a living had to be met. There was little Louis Kissinger could do at the outset, being unfamiliar with English and consequently unable to teach. He eventually found himself a clerical job; the boys were enrolled in schools and Paula became the family breadwinner.

Her superb talents in the kitchen saved their lives. She first joined a catering firm but, as her fame grew, Paula more or less went into business on her own. She catered cocktail parties and other social affairs, being recommended from one to the other to the point where she eventually could pick and choose her clients.

Enrolled at George Washington High School, Heinz, who Americanized his name to Henry, quickly overcame the language barrier. He was fifteen and English came naturally to him even if he has remained haunted by an accent. Why he hasn't lost it is something of a mystery for, by all the rules of linguistics, he was at the right age to pick up an unemcumbered command of the language.

Kissinger admits to being self-conscious about it, and for years he refused to speak on television. Fellow diplomats stand in awe of his English but deplore what they called his "Bavarian accent." Then, there are cynics who maintain that, like Charles Boyer's and Maurice Chevalier's, Kissinger's accent grew more pronounced with the years—because women found it attractive. That makes sense, for Kissinger, if anything, is a consummate showman and no slouch when it comes to compensating for his early shy lonely years in his adopted country.

In Germany Henry had been only an average student, but in America his genius began to show. "Positively glow," was how one teacher, Martha Horowitz Shiff described it. The late Mrs. Shiff, wife of Dr. Nathan Shiff, a New York physician and writer, taught history at George Washington. Young Henry was one of her pupils. "Martha and I weren't married then," Dr. Shiff recalled. "We were dating, and night after night I would have to hear about this brilliant refugee boy. Martha told me how he asked questions that sent her scurrying to the text books to make sure she had come up with the right answer. 'There was something inexhaustible about his curiosity,' she told me. He never seemed satisfied with the answers she gave, that there was always something more to be found out. He had a passion for facts.

"Martha, though, always pointed out the quality of his manners. Smart kids have a way of being overbearing. Smug and superior—out to get the teacher, to show her up. There was nothing of that in Henry Kissinger. He was deadly serious about his thirst for knowledge. He wanted to know because he needed to know. Martha remembered him as a Straight A student whose authority in English seemed to leap forward by the hour."

After Henry found a day-time job with a shaving brush company he switched to night school—a challenge that defeats ninety percent of the enrollees. Not Henry. His grades stayed high.

With his sense of the dramatic Kissinger today claims that he was paid fifteen dollars a week. The man who hired him remembered it as being closer to thirty-five, at least when he moved swiftly up from messenger to shipping clerk after graduating from High School and enrolling at the City College of New York. His ambition then was to be an accountant. "For a refugee it was an easy profession to get into," he said. Speaking of those first years in the work force Kissinger views them philosophically, "It wasn't a hardship, working my way through school. We had a very close family relationship and things didn't seem that hard to

38

me. I was not brought up to have a lot of leisure; there was no shame in that."

By the time Henry was in his late teens, he was a tough young man. And practical. In a sense he had made out on his own. The family helped, but had Henry been dropped into the middle of Washington Heights the chances are that he would have reached precisely the same point that he found himself on the eve of Pearl Harbor in December, 1941. Working at a grubby job, taking night courses to improve himself, planning for a career within his range of the moment and going with a girl, Anneliese Fleischer.

Like Henry, Ann was a refugee from nearby Nuremberg. She was easily the prettiest girl in the crowd Henry went with, composed largely of young German exiles, and she might have chosen any of them for her "steady." But she found Henry appealing. His shyness attracted her, so did his soulful eyes, the "little boy lost" quality that belied his inner toughness. Ann wasn't looking for toughness in Henry, so she didn't find it. He was anything but a swinger then. How could he be? With so little time and money.

Among the young refugees, many of whom had received their "Greetings" from Uncle Sam, there was little surprise in Pearl Harbor. "We weren't normal Americans," a refugee friend of Kissinger recalled. "We had none of that American feeling —'It can't happen to us. They won't attack America.' We had seen it happen. We were there. We were prepared to die in the war, either by war action or as a result of the war. Because we expected Hitler to win.

"We thought America would lose the war because we remembered the times in Germany when we couldn't cross the streets for six days because there were so many tanks rolling by. I'm pretty sure Henry felt the same way, that he expected Hitler to win."

Henry's "Greetings" arrived shortly before his twentieth birthday. Going off to war was quite the "in" thing socially in those pre-Korea and pre-Viet Nam days, what seems now to have been a naive, almost medieval era. There were parties for the inductees and going-away presents galore. Any young man could expect at least a half dozen sewing kits and an equal number of identity bracelets. Henry's festivities were climaxed by a party given at the old Iceland, a large catering hall near Times Square on February 6, 1943, with a photographer present to record the event for future generations.

Photographs show a curly-haired young man, chubby, with a long, strong chin, frame glasses, even teeth, rich lips and an ingratiating smile. One could imagine a pretty, intelligent girl like Ann Fleischer being interested in him and probably more than willing to promise to wait. How sincerely Henry was committed to her remained another question. Both young people were caught up in their own past, thrown together by their common loneliness, the realization that they were "outsiders" in an alien world. Their families knew each other and everyone around them admired and respected the friendship. A lot was taken for granted about the relationship that perhaps did not exist—or should not have presumed to exist in the first place.

But, then, 1943 was hardly the time to ponder the unforseeable future. Henry and Ann knew all about uncertainty. They'd lived enough of it in their two decades on earth, and now they would be experiencing more of the same. Unlike native-born Americans they lacked the faith to be sure that "Henry would come marching home again." Their world was colored by deep-rooted cynicism born of real experience. They knew better than to trust the future. Their problem lay in survival.

All the circumstances were right for the war and his Army duty to combine in making Henry Kissinger destiny's son. Lady Luck was right there, riding with him all the way, and any Broadway handicapper could have picked him as a winner from the beginning. For the first time that accent came in handy. It gave him an aura of distinction setting him apart from the other G.I.'s Of course, he was bright. And he was a loner—the guy who didn't mix. You may not get to be a general that way—but you're bound to get somewhere. You're different—and the Army has to do something about you.

Henry's mind showed up in his army tests—something that didn't happen to everybody. Those stories about potential atomic scientists ending up in the Quartermaster Corps were all too true, but even when Pvt. Henry was "busted" from intellect to infantryman he remained an odds-on favorite.

At first Henry was selected for the Army Special Training Program and was assigned a two-year engineering program at Lafayette College in Easton, Pennsylvania, only eighty miles from home. But after only two semesters the Army abruptly terminated its college program. Casualties were mounting in Europe and the Pacific, and fresh troops were needed. He was shipped to Camp Claiborne, Louisiana, and shaped into a combat infantryman.

It was a summer morning and Henry was deep into training—trudging along a road on maneuvers. A Jeep pulled up alongside the sweating regiment, just as they were given a few minutes at ease. The men sprawled to the ground in a state of exhaustion and Henry had just closed his eyes, expecting to grab some sleep, when he heard a loudspeaker going full blast and turned toward the noise where he witnessed one of the more incredible sights the Army was offering that year—a PFC with a monocle dangling over his uniform. Like Kissinger the soldier had an accent and there he was—standing in the jeep telling the soldiers why they were fighting the war. It was brief, curt and clear, very Prussian, Kissinger thought. This man, whoever he was, was a no-nonsense guy.

The PFC was Fritz Kraemer, at the time thirty-five years old, scion of a prominent Protestant family that for generations held title to a considerable estate along the Rhine. Kraemer had just acquired a Ph.D at the Goethe University at Frankfurt when Hitler came to power. A man of action he stormed out of Germany, letting anyone who would listen to him know why. In Rome he picked up another degree and then came to America where he enlisted in the U.S. Army as his personal answer to Pearl Harbor. Kraemer organized a military-government school for the officers and men of the 84th Division. Part of his duty, he felt, was letting the soldiers in the field know why they were there. And that was why he was there— monocle, Prussian manner, German accent and all.

Kissinger was deeply impressed and the next day he wrote him a note:, "Dear Private Kraemer: I heard you speak yesterday. This is how it should be done. Can I help you somehow?"

Kraemer had touched a chord in the young man. Having searched his own conscience for the answers to Nazism he could speak profoundly about the moral necessity of fighting Hitler. He obviously had articulated what young Henry himself was feeling.

Henry's letter flattered the brilliant older man and he willingly arranged for a meeting. Kraemer later explained that he saw Kissinger because of the letter's simplicity. "There were no frills. Just thought. This was a man of discipline and initiative."

Kraemer recalled the meeting as exhilarating. "Henry was a natural phenomenon. He had the urgent desire not to understand superficial things, but the underlying causes. He wanted to grasp things." Kraemer was impressed with his intellectual cool and the short conversation, not more than twenty minutes, convinced him that he had met one of the best minds he had ever encountered. What astonished him most was Henry's youthfulness.

This was how Fritz Kraemer, now a special Pentagon advisor at the Pentagon, still wearing his monocle and as loud and opinionated as ever, became Henry Kissinger's "discoverer" an attribution he wishes had never been started. "I was merely the catalyst for a mind that already existed."

The meeting turned out to be enormously fruitful for young Henry. Kraemer became Henry's sponsor during his Army career and afterward. He cultivated the young man's intellect as carefully as his own. He realized he had met someone totally unique—a man with a sixth sense of historical dimensions. He unhesitatingly told Kissinger what he thought of him, "You are unbelievably gifted."

The impression Kissinger made on Kraemer paid off but for the first year of their friendship, Kissinger remained a rifleman. In December, 1944, he crouched in a frozen foxhole near Bastogne, in Belgium, beside Pvt. Antoun Mudarri, of Syrian descent, who is now a Boston rug merchant. He remembered Kissinger's extraordinary cool when the German artillery drew closer. With the Battle of the Bulge raging all around them, Henry said, "Tony, the best place for us would be that hayloft over there, because it's warm. If we have to get killed, we'll get killed anyway. So let's have a good sleep."

They headed for the hayloft, burrowed themselves in it and proceeded to sit down and discuss world affairs. The battle raged on around them—and without them. Until they both had rested and went back to the business of waging war.

Kraemer kept plugging for Kissinger and when the 84th moved into Germany Henry was made German-speaking interpreter for the commanding general in the closing months of the war. In March, 1945, at the age of twenty-one, promoted to Sergeant, he was abruptly put in charge of the shattered city of Krefeld with a population of 180,000 with orders to get it functioning again.

"I could only marvel," recalled Kraemer. "In just two or three days, the government was working again, in a splendid fashion. Henry had planned things wonderfully. There had been nothing—not a telephone, no food, nothing. How did Henry know what to do? There is no cookbook for seducing a woman—you can either do it or not. He went about it ice-cold, with total objectivity. He said, 'All right, we have to get the water works back in order. Who was the water works engineer?' They said, 'He was a Nazi.' And Henry said, 'All right, who was the engineer before the Nazis came. Get him.' "

Kissinger made such an impression on the Army brass that it seemed he was involved in doing everything everywhere—getting town after town, district after district, back into working order.

In Bensheim, a hillside town of 17,000 people in the West German state of Hesse, he is remembered with awe, admiration and affection. "We don't want any articles about the 'dark side of Henry Kissinger' to come out of here," a City Father told a reporter recently. "That man is very respected here." And true enough, the townspeople in Bensheim hold him in the highest esteem. Only seven years before his arrival, Kissinger and his family had fled as Jewish refugees from Fuerth, a little more than a hundred miles to the east. "I remember," said his former secretary, Frau Elisabeth Heid, "that he used to say: 'We have not come here to take revenge.' You know, in those days after the war, this sort of attitude was far from taken for granted."

He rode into town behind the wheel of a gleaming white 1938 Mercedes-Benz which he had confiscated from a Nazi factory owner. He made his way through the narrow streets of the old town to the tax office, bounded up the steps as he nodded to a German guard, "I'm Mister Henry from the Counter-Intelligence Corps and I'm taking over this floor."

Said another old resident of the city, "He took over the largest hillside villa in a posh suburb which used to be called Adolf Hitler. You could see him every Sunday at the soccer matches. He was zealous in rounding up Bensheim's Nazis and he stuck strictly to the rules. He was completely self-assured and exuded so much authority that even his American friends would never dare to put their feet on the desk in his office."

A single thread runs through Henry Kissinger's life—taking advantage of the right situation and making the most of it. This may be a simplisitic clue to his diplomatic legerdemain. Until Henry returned to Germany, got promoted to Sergeant, landed the job of top man, commandant of the CIC detachment in Bensheim, the best one can dig up about his celebrated interest in women is that he lost his virginity when he was about fifteen and still in Germany, which hardly ranks as an international achievement.

He was supposed also to have been involved in a puppy love affair with a girl his own age whose family disapproved of him—until they got to know the short, fuzzy-haired, plump young boy a little better. The girl's mother was the first to fall under the spell of his charm; the father gave in when he started talking to Heinz and perceived his intelligence.

Young Heinz looked on in horror one night when a band of marauding Storm Troopers, spurred by a violent anti-Semitic address in Fuerth by notorious Jew-baiter Julius Streicher, rammed open the door of the neighboring family's home, piled in with torches and pillaged it. Hours after they left the bloody, ravaged bodies of the parents and the young girl where carried uncovered, dripping with blood, to a filthy truck where they were dumped like so much waste.

Then in Washington Heights there was his friendship with Ann Fleischer. That about represents the young man's private life and we can only assume that once in the Army he did what comes naturally to soldiers, enjoying various ladies without committing himself to even the occasional postcard.

Henry, though, blossomed in the Bensheim suburb where he had commandeered a villa. There was nothing ontoward about it. That was his right as commandant, fellow soldiers recalled. A friend remembered how Kissinger really thrived on his role of boss. Like others in Intelligence he got around the ruling against fraternization with Germans on the grounds that his job entailed obtaining information and how did one get information without talking to the people? That females seemed to be more popular as sources than males was merely a happy coincidence.

Henry's metamorphosis from dullard to swinging commandant resulted in a bright household at the villa. He and his buddies chipped in to hire a maid and a housekeeper, and the ladies had their work cut out for them—cleaning up after the boss' parties which his friends described as "fabulous."

The "boss" knew how to "liberate" the best of everything—good whiskey, fine food, and beautiful women. "Especially that blonde who lived with him," said a friend of those cheery days. "She was a knockout—a real beauty."

The girl was supposed to have been the young widow of a Wehrmacht officer, and that would account for her style. There were other women in young Henry's life and another fellow volunteered, "I give him credit for one thing. If he wanted to go out with a girl he liked, he went out with her. He didn't care what anyone said. He always did his job and did it well. So no one could say he was carousing around and ducking his work. He did his job, but he always found the time to get around.

"The way I figured it out Henry must have been a slow starter, the kind of guy who wanted things to be right—or not at all. He didn't fool around much until he got that great job. Then he went to town—like some fellow who just discovered there was such a thing as a woman. He'd stake out the most luscious beauties available and then started dazzling them. He didn't stop at anything. His job helped, of course. But the Sergeant had technique. He'd send flowers, get the girls to the villa for lunch. He was pretty straightforward about everything. They all knew what he was up to, and once he scored, Henry hooked them. For a funny-looking fellow with glasses he left a lot of broken hearts behind.

"Henry was a gentleman when it came to girls. He had lots of charm and, of course, he spoke the language. Those German girls dug him."

With Henry Kissinger's prominence have come legends, myths that have some basis in fact but others prove to have been made up of whole cloth. Sergeant Henry, for example, appears now in the history of the German occupation as the regional commandant who grabbed up hidden Nazis as though they were flies drawn to flypaper.

One of the favorite stories about Kissinger tells of how he put up posters in Bensheim advertising for men with "police experience" and requesting them to report for headquarters for jobs. "The Gestapo people," he said, "turned up by the dozen. I landed more Gestapo agents than the entire rest of the U.S. Army."

Actually, advertising for "police help" was a common CIC ploy to route out Nazis and there was nothing original about it. Similarly, old Army men downgrade Kissinger's aplomb in taking over his suburban villa, peopling it with beautiful ladies and "liberating" fine food and wine to stock its cellar. "It was common practice for CIC agents to pick up the best houses, and the best women in town," said one scornful veteran of the 84th Division. "It doesn't mean a damned thing when everybody does it."

With his success in the Army assured and increased responsibility facing him Henry might easily have become a big-headed lout. "He wasn't"—this from a soldier who served with him.

"In town after town he was literally the head of state—the Supreme Commander. His word was law, but he never abused privileges. Any other yokel would have gone beserk at that stage with so much authority.

"Henry Kissinger's cool was astonishing. I marvelled at it then—when I was so much younger. Now, I don't believe it ever happened. He was friendly but correct with all of us, bright, smiling, good-humored. He shared whatever he had. He handled the local people with superb tact. Being German-born may have helped, but no one, either German or American, ever stepped out of line."

Kissinger transferred out in April, 1946, to take a teaching post at the European Command Intelligence School located in Oberammergau, home of the *Bavarian Passion Play* and seat of deep-rooted, ancient anti-Semitism. Fritz Kraemer, now a lieutenant, was on the faculty there, instructing field-grade officers how to flush Nazis from the underground havens. By no means the top man at the school, Kraemer was, as always, flamboyant and colorful. He was an American lieutenant wearing a monocle and carrying a swagger stick. One of the faculty said, "He was slightly mad and absolutely wonderful."

He may have been mad, low man on the totem pole, but Kraemer packed influence and when he recommended Kissinger as a lecturer he told the commandant, "I want you to take a man who has nothing but a high school diploma and some work in a brush factory in New York. If he doesn't work out you can assign him to the wood-gathering detail."

Kissinger arrived and was immediately success-
ful, teaching a course on the "structure of the
Nazi state," basing his lectures on books and reports that Kraemer gave him. It was a feat of
memory as much as anything else.

Four days before his twenty-third birthday
Henry was mustered out of the Army and joined
the school as a civilian, earning ten thousand dollars a year and a captain's rank in the reserve.

The kid who had once walked on the other side
of the street in Fuerth to avoid getting beat up
and worked his way through high school in a loft
on West Twenty-third Street in New York and
who had gotten no further parchment-wise in his
education than a high school diploma had a lot
going for him.

His military awards included the Bronze Stars
and two letters of commendation. Now, in his civilian career, he was seeing more money than he
had ever knew existed. So was Walter Kissinger.
He had taken his discharge in the Pacific, remaining in Seoul for an extra year—as a War Department foreign service officer. The motivation was
similar to his brother's—there was no money in
the family.

Kraemer began to worry about his protege as
Henry lived it up. Oberammergau was a playground Henry knew well, close to the Bavarian
Alps whose hospices offered all sorts of weekend
diversion. Then there was nearby Munich,
bombed-out but still a fun town for a soldier on
leave. Henry acquired a fine roster of feminine
companions and began giving the impression of a
young man out for a good time—something to

51

compensate for the privations of his youth.

The failure of the Kissinger brothers to return immediately to Washington Heights at the end of the war caused more than raised eyebrows. Paula and Louis Kissinger understood their need for money, but even with less than their sons were earning they could all get along and the boys would have the opportunity to continue their educations.

But there were those who couldn't fathom the young men's reasoning—or their indifference. Walter's fiancee broke her engagement and Ann Fleischer abruptly quit college and left New York. She went to Colorado. Her friends were mystified. One said, "For a single girl to go so far away from home didn't make sense. It was as though she deliberately wanted to put as many miles between her and Washington Heights as she could. Maybe she was searching for something out there."

Kraemer's fears proved groundless. He hadn't "adopted" a playboy. Henry had just been experimenting and ten grand a year hadn't lulled him into the feeling that this was all there was to life. There were a lot more brass rings on the Merry-Go-Round, and he intended picking them off. He had long since forgotten that the ultimate of his ambitions had been to become an accountant.

Young Henry had savored the joy of success—the satisfaction of accomplishing new, untried tasks and winning approval for his efforts. He was no longer the shy kid who had left New York for the Army, frightened, worried about his life more than his future, doubtful that the America he knew so little about could beat the might of Hitler

—which had so mercilessly beaten his father and might too have beaten him and Walter—except for the accident of their youth.

Henry told Kraemer, "All I know is what I teach at school. I have to go home. I need to have a first class education."

Kraemer, ever the snob, warned the young man, "You will be like most New Yorkers—provincial. You'll study at one of the local colleges. It's easy and convenient. But, Henry, a gentleman does not go to a local New York school."

Henry listened.

When Henry returned to New York in 1947, he was twenty-three years old, mature beyond his years, thanks to his extraordinary intellect and experiences. It was a heady world he tumbled into—from a nobody private just like anyone else—except for that accent—into an adroit respected military administrator and finally a teacher making as much money as many professors of the era earned in the prime of their lives.

But things had not changed substantially in Washington Heights. Paula was still in the catering business and Louis Kissinger plodded away at his job. He had hung on every word from his son about conditions in Germany. It had not been ten years since Louis Kissinger fled his country, but for someone of his age, inclinations and personality, they added up to a lifetime. He longed to go back —just for a visit. There was no thought of picking up the pieces again and starting over. At sixty Kissinger was too old for foolish dreams.

Then there was Ann who had returned when Henry did. She had changed little in the six years Henry had stormed the heights. As always she was demure, pleasant, eager to please, grateful for any nice things that happened to her. To those close to Ann in the war years, there wasn't the slightest doubt that she had remained faithful to Henry and that, given the opportunity to accept, she would certainly agree to marriage. Nothing else had ever entered her mind.

Paula and Louis Kissinger were not the kind of parents who wanted their son safely locked in the arms of a wife who would "take care of him" and the sparse information one can uncover about the Fleischers suggests that they too were inclined to leave the young to their own devices. Enough for them to cope with exile, building a new life, enduring a war—and now looking forward in the twilight of their lives to that elusive intangible called peace.

The lessons of World War I were fresh enough in America's mind to make certain veterans of War Number Two got something resembling a decent break. There was the *52-50 Club* which permitted ex-soldiers to draw fifty dollars a week in benefits for a year. There was a bonus payment upon discharge, the G.I. Bill of Rights covered a lot of territory, and its educational provisions were the most exciting. You could study everything from ballroom dancing to Yoga. You could become a circus acrobat, a veterinarian, or a medical doctor, lawyer, maybe, even an Indian chief. Kissinger chose political science and Harvard offered him a scholarship.

The prestigious university hadn't represented the culmination of his life's ambitions. He accepted it pragmatically, as every other step in his life, another move ahead. The immediate post-war years made for a wonderful period in higher education. Eager, excited minds were at work on college campuses—minds, like Kissinger's, older than the average freshman and contemptuous of the frivolities of the old-guard gold fish gulping undergraduate. At Harvard the opportunities to exercise mental agility were especially exciting—and Henry Kissinger went at the challenges of the university with characteristic bulldog energy and enthusiasm.

Kissinger's maturity was almost complete. His Intelligence experience had sharpened qualities inherent in his character. There were advantages to being taciturn, introspective. These were Kissinger qualities to cultivate. He had been on the inside of power politics—however small the level. He had watched political power at work. He liked what he had seen. He wanted a broader view, a wider platform.

When the average young American dreams of fame and fortune he imagines it either in terms of reward for his own efforts or facetiously as the payoff for marrying the boss' daughter. He does not look for a patron. This is the European way. Kissinger has always been able to find a patron at significant points in his own life. In the Army it was Kraemer; at Harvard, his mentor turned out to be William Yandall Elliott, an irascible Professor of Government who was enormously fashionable at the time. To many, the Southern educator was a bore, an autocrat who shuttled between Cambridge and Washington where he was consultant to the House Foreign Affairs Committee.

He was fifty at the time, staunchly anti-Communist and dedicated to the belief that America's role in world affairs was that of undebatable leader. Elliott enjoyed a cult, of course, but there were many on campus who could live without his pomposity and arrogance. They did not include Henry Kissinger who affected Elliott in much the same manner that he impressed Kraemer. There was instant rapport between the two men and except for the difference in their ages, it became difficult to distinguish between teacher and pupil. Henry, at the outset, impressed fellow students more as a youngish teacher than a colleague.

Henry created a base for himself within Elliott's orbit and enjoyed especially his pithy comments on the scene in Washington which he knew intimately as well as inside fragments about what was happening politically in Europe, especially his tales of Konrad Adenauer, then Chancellor of West Germany. Elliott was a skilled raconteur who, more than Kraemer, inspired the respect of his protege, whose wit and humor were still a long way from finding an audience. As a student Henry Kissinger wasn't the kind of fellow who got "rushed."

Henry, characteristically, assumed the role of loner, the aloof scholar, the fellow who spoke only when spoken to. He gave what energies he could spare from his studies to Professor Elliott, helping him with administrative work and generally making himself useful. Elliott and fellow professors adored Henry but Harvard students vetoed him. They took a dim view of the way he buttered up not only Elliott but the professor's chief rival for attention, Professor Carl Friedrich. A "special" student was supposed to be the exclusivity of one or the other. Kissinger managed to find support among both for what he was now apparently taking seriously—his genius.

"It was bound to happen," said one former classmate. "After all he was only twenty-three, and he'd been acting forty-three for so long in the Army that I guess he had to break down and be an SOB. To know him was to loathe him. He walked around expecting everyone to notice him because he was extraordinary—a fat, pudgy lump of 'extraordinariness' with that awful accent.

"Henry hadn't a good word for anyone—unless he was in a position to do him some good. So that eliminated all the students. None of us lived in Henry's rarefied atmosphere and he'd have to wait, at least until after graduation, before we could be considered valuable.

"He was terribly insecure, I guess. Harvard just wasn't geared for a refugee with so many American credentials. He was the kind of hybrid who couldn't have pleased everybody even if he tried. Maybe, with his practical way of looking at things, he figured that out for himself. Yet it's a shame in a way. A man in his position ought to be able to enjoy the feedback of some gentler reactions to his college days than Henry does. He came closer to self objectivity I imagine when success finally tapped him I guess he can afford to be a human being now."

Perhaps his fellow students misjudged Henry. The anecdotes from his Army years are sprinkled with charm and good humor. It does not seem possible that he could have undergone such drastic a personality change, but, besides his studies, there were other things on his mind. One of them was marriage; the other was being forged, Kissinger's flirtation with the CIA and espionage. For all his intellect he was still a young man play-acting, and holding himself aloof from the entanglements of campus life surrounded him with an air of mystery. Another famous German, Marlene Dietrich, often said, "There's no harm being a little unpopular or difficult. It makes you interesting."

Of his first days at Harvard, Kissinger said, "I had gotten out of the Army and I felt like an immigrant again. When I went into the Army I was a refugee, and when I got out I was an immigrant."

He was assigned to Calvery Hall, the most dilapidated dormitory on the campus and shared a two-bedroom suite with Arthur Gillman, of Boston, and Edward Mendel, a New Yorker, both Jewish. This was how Harvard made its room assignments.

Said Gillman, "Henry was different from the other veterans. He worked harder, studied more. He'd read until two or three in the morning. He had tremendous drive and discipline. He spent a lot of time thinking. He was absorbing everything."

Not everyone was impressed. "He was secretive," said an old schoolmate who preferred to be anonymous, "He sat in that overstuffed chair—the kind Harvard rooms were full of—studying from morning until night and biting his nails, till there was blood." (Kissinger still bites his nails).

"He played the German scholar to the hilt," continued the anonymous observer, "wearing the same clothes all the time—for at least two years. What with his scholarship and the G.I. bill he wasn't all that broke—and his parents not that great much in need that he was sending them every dollar so he could say one day that he studied by candlelight. Kissinger struck me as being a poseur—someone who for periods of his life acted one role and then turned around and played out another part.

"I got this impression from the way he talked about his Army life. He was a different Kissinger. Bright, amusing, fascinating. And sometimes he even had charm—something I always found missing when he was at Harvard. Yet, they insist the Secretary of State spreads charm around these days like it was manure."

Henry, when pressed, would recall some of his amorous exploits in Germany, but at that point he stopped. He showed no evidence of interest in the girls available at nearby Radcliffe and women seldom came into his conversation—except as abstractions. He sometimes would propound his thesis that women should be compelled to ingratiate themselves to those in authority, that they really wanted to live in this manner.

His Jewish fellow-students, understandably curious about his childhood in Nazi Germany, found few of their questions answered. They were led to believe that Nazi persecutions at the time were no more profound than the everyday anti-Semitism Jews met in America. Kissinger avoided recalling Fuerth and limited his German anecdotes to those involving his Intelligence work.

Despite what some felt was his lack of charm, Kissinger was beginning to feel his oats as a raconteur. Perhaps Elliott's influences were starting to manifest themselves. In the dormitory, when he could be coaxed away from his books, Kissinger became much in demand as a teller of tales—tall and otherwise. The students found him fascinating—and mysterious—which was the way he wanted it.

They were surprised, for instance, to discover that he had a brother. Walter's name had never been mentioned until the young man showed up one day at Harvard and was introduced around. And until she appeared as Mrs. Henry Kissinger, few ever heard of Ann Fleischer either.

What astonished the Harvard most about Henry was that such a young man had become a hardliner. They could understand his loathing of Nazism but there were no rational explanations for his paranoia about Russia. He didn't seem like an Establishment person, yet he belonged to the school that looked under the bed every night, fearful of a Soviet spy. This could have been Elliott, but Kissinger's Russian devils were very real. He talked constantly about how naive Americans were in respect to awareness of the menace of international Communism.

Another thing bothered his Harvard classmates. Henry never griped—and for a man with his Army experience this didn't make sense. He accepted life in the decrepit dormitory casually and the monotonous cafeteria food appeared not to bother him at all. "There was nothing normal about Henry," said a friend. "He didn't have the childish, stupid reactions to anything that belonged in the character of a student. No kid anymore—but still a student."

When Ann Fleischer and Henry Kissinger were in their teens they shared many things. They were refugees making their way in a strange country, both serious, intellectually inclined. Ann realized quickly her mind was no match for Henry's, but that was to be expected. She was, after all, a European young woman and no one in the Forties paid much attention to the stirrings of Women's Lib. Still, a woman of her background and with opportunities available was expected to get an education.

Her grades at George Washington High School disappointed her. Ann's average was seventy-nine and her scholarship dipped further when she attended Hunter College. Still, Ann doggedly pursued education. She audited Hunter courses and during the war years she worked hard at her studies, despite the illness of her father and numerous other family problems.

There was no reason to explain Ann's abrupt departure for Colorado. It could have been Henry's failure to return from Germany, the family situation—or both. Her sister, Lenore, believed that it had something to do with her childhood memories of Bavaria. "We were hooked on Switzerland," she said. "We lived so close, in Bavaria, and we used to spend every holiday there. It was the only chance under Hitler to get a breath of fresh air."

Ann entered the University of Colorado in Boulder and on weekends she worked as a waitress at the Broadmoor Hotel. When she came back to New York about the time that Henry left Oberammergau the old relationship appeared, on the surface at least, to take up where it had left off.

That they were two vastly different people must have occurred to them. They were too bright and intelligent to ignore the fact. Enough of their European heritage, however, had rubbed off to make them creatures of habit. They were used to each other and marriage might make them comfortable if not more interesting. Henry had always fascinated Ann and there was as much hero-worship in her devotion as genuine affection.

In late 1948, with Elliott's help, Kissinger received a fifteen-hundred-a-year, teaching fellowship. He also won a prized Detur Scholarship. Since his schedule was so heavy that he couldn't work, the money was vital. It meant that now they could be married.

It was a lot different from the series of farewell parties that preceded Henry's induction into the Army. There were no announcements around the campus—no fanfare, just a simple wedding during the mid-term break, Frebruary, 1949.

The Orthodox ceremony, held at the Kissinger home, was performed by a rabbi whom a guest described as "so Orthodox that he refused to recognize the secular government of Israel." The strictness of the ceremony, requiring Ann to take the ritual bath (the *mikvah*) before the ceremony, annoyed Henry who considered himself a "liberated man." Only a few intimate friends attended and they included none of the refugees the family had known from Fuerth and Nuremberg. No one from Harvard. If an explanation were offered it seemed to be saying that the wedding had been deliberately small and informal because of the illness of the bride's father which precluded the usual festivities.

There was no honeymoon as the newlyweds headed for Newton Center, near Cambridge, Massachusetts, where Henry had rented a small apartment. It was all new to Ann who had visited Henry only once or twice on campus. "She seemed demure, like a frightened doe," said Henry's anonymous classmate. "You'd never believe they had just married. They were completely undemonstrative. There wasn't the usual give and take you find between people—especially a young bride and groom. It was hard to explain because it was the sort of thing I'd never seen before—or since. They never touched. They never communicated. Ann seemed like an appurtenance—another 'something' that Henry had around to go with his baggy clothes, his stacks of papers, his spectacles.

"Henry had been more devoted to the dog that accompanied him on his first trip to Harvard. Because he risked the wrath of the maid who cleaned the place, Henry took the dog to a kennel every morning, picked it up every evening and brought it back to the apartment where they spent the evening together. It was like a ritual, never changing until the dog died."

If the marriage lacked lustre emotionally it proved eminently satisfying as a matter of practicality—certainly for Henry. Ann was a good cook and she began fattening up the young man whose preoccupation with studies had led him into casual eating habits. She had learned bookkeeping from her brother-in-law and took a full-time job in a furniture store. She also typed Henry's papers including his massive senior honors thesis which ran over seven hundred pages. Recalls sister Lenore, "Ann worked very hard. She really made it possible for Henry to complete his education."

No matter how generously one considers Henry Kissinger's marriage to Ann Fleischer, the unsubtle evidence points to an out-and-out union of convenience. Henry needed someone to take care of his personal needs. Ann was handy, convenient, hopelessly hooked on him. Why not grab the opportunity while it lay there? There would be consequences—as there always are—in such cold-blooded arrangements, but Kissinger, for all his brilliance, like many frosty intellectual men, either chose not to foresee them or swept them under the rug.

So here he was at Harvard, acknowledged a brilliant student, absorbed in his work with Dr. Elliott, working on his papers, his domestic needs beautifully managed, and ready to embark on undercover activities for the Government. Henry would have his first taste of cloak-and-dagger work.

In 1951, Henry became involved in the Harvard International Seminars set up by Elliott with Henry as executive director. To the Harvard Establishment they were just another divertisement, but the seminars succeeded wildly, attracting six hundred participants from thirty countries all over the world. Their major purpose was to counteract Soviet propaganda by means of influencing young opinion makers. Each summer forty invitations were sent to rising young academics, government officials, journalists and artists, the emphasis being on youth. Henry had begun to enjoy the power of fooling around with other people's minds—and other people's countries. He may not have realized it at the time but he was attracting the very ambitious, very intense people who someday he could call on as the leader of a government.

One of Kissinger's seminarians in 1954 was Valery Giscard, then twenty-eight, now president of France. In 1957 there came Yigal Allon, later deputy premier of Israel. Then there was Erhard Eppler who became West German Minister for Economic Cooperation and Lep Tindemans, Belgium's prospective premier and Norway's future foreign minister, Knut Frydenlund.

Obviously the Seminar attracted extraordinary young people and superficially the *Think Tank* appeared to be a rousing success—an open-and-above board international meeting of young minds that Harvard, Elliott and Kissinger could be proud of.

That the money came from the Ford Foundation gave the seminars a certain suspicious smell that was offset by the participation of another group, the Rockefeller-backed Asia Foundation. Nelson Rockefeller, then going through his liberal phase, had become an excellent handy front man for the Rockefeller investments. Looking like *Mr. Clean* and acting like any ordinary guy, the billionaire who turned "Hi ya fella" into a common-touch trademark, Rocky's public service record contributed much toward diminishing the Rockefeller image of a vast conglomerate protecting its vested interests whatever the cost in human misery or political double-crossing. Rocky covered beautifully for the international manipulations that remained constant in the Rockefeller bag of dirty tricks.

The funding of the Harvard Seminars also invited the participation of individuals and small groups like the innocent sounding Friends of the Middle East. No one paid much attention to reports that, alone of all the participants, the Friends of the Middle East took a firm hand in deciding which Arab seminarians were considered the opinion-makers of the future and which were not. One tolerates that sort of thing in the academic world—where money is money and the "Board" has to be satisfied.

The New York Times eventually identified the Friends of the Middle East as a front for the CIA —a state of affairs that horrified Kissinger. "God, this is terrible." He moaned to his friends, "People will think I was working with the CIA."

He was.

When a Turkish student, a Fellow at the Seminars, died under mysterious circumstances, his diary revealed that Kissinger had attempted to lure him into the CIA fold as a "political observer." Kissinger also carefully weeded out Communists and young people with Leftist leanings. The final screening of participants in the seminar was left to Kissinger's judgment by Elliott and the Seminar's administration. He enjoyed a comparatively free hand—and thrived on the authority.

Kissinger weathered out the CIA storm which amused most of the Europeans who couldn't conceive of such a vast international project being sponsored without government funding—secret or otherwise. Said a young Italian, "It's only you Americans who start out with the concept of political virginity."

The Seminars spread much good will for the Kissinger name—and respect—among Government institutions, especially the sneaky ones. Kissinger fulfilled various secret assignments for Army Intelligence which had won congratulations of his superiors, and now he had ingratiated himself with the upper echelon of the CIA. With only a B.A. in hand, he became a consultant to the Army's Operation Research Office in Washington. In 1951 he was sent to Korea and later reminisced, "I knew absolutely nothing about Korea." He also knew nothing about centuries-old Korean-Japanese hostility, because he stopped in Japan to get letters of recommendation. "For the first two weeks in Korea," he said, "no one would see me."

Kissinger had made his auspicious entrance into the world of power, politics and diplomacy, and he could be grateful to the Harvard International Seminars. They demonstrated the potential of a theory that is as old as politics itself—the concept of a Grand Council of giant intellects charged with managing the destiny of a nation.

A decade or so ago, perhaps even against the secrecy of the Johnson administration, Americans would have whooped with laughter at the recent report that President Gerald Ford, like Richard Nixon in the impotent two years of his second administration, governs in the grip of Henry Kissinger and a secret group of forty intellectuals he heads and who meet regularly to determine America's foreign and domestic policy.

Now, we know better. *It Can Happen Here.* It's already happened.

Daniel Ellsberg is one man who believes America's Secret Government does exist and Henry Kissinger is the real Mr. President.

Cracks began to appear in Henry's scholastic shell as he settled down into married life and work toward his advanced degrees. Henry and Ann moved to Cambridge and he acquired a battered second-hand car. They took to inviting friends in for dinner and became popular campus hosts, possibly because what Ann couldn't maneuver in the kitchen her mother could. Mrs. Fleischer frequently visited the couple and helped out. The dinners were sumptuous by collegiate standards—sit-down affairs and beautifully prepared.

Money remained in short supply since the young couple were totally dependent on Henry's academic income and Ann's take-home pay as a bookkeeper. Said Ann's sister, Lenore Reich, "But they worked hard together. They had no leisure. Sometimes, it's easier when you don't have time to think about things."

Henry, certainly, had little spare time. When it came to his academic output, Henry Kissinger didn't kid around. For his undergraduate thesis, presented in 1950 and titled *The Meaning of History—Reflections on Spengzer, Toynbee and Kant*, Kissinger's reflections on the three philosophers ran to more than three hundred and fifty pages. Ann typed them and Dr. Elliott, they said, read only the first hundred, quit there and gave Henry a *summa cum laude*. A decree was handed down, as a result of Kissinger's king-size dissertation, that henceforth Government Department theses at Harvard had to pack it all in within one hundred and fifty pages.

Contemporary Kissinger biographers have shown understandable restraint about reading the thesis for clues to the Kissinger character, choosing to rely on campus gossip of the period. "The writing style was ponderous. Henry was still thinking in German and the essay read like quickly translated German," said an Elliott colleague. "But young Kissinger could do no wrong in those palmy days. He corrected the teacher's papers, wrote large chunks of Elliott's own papers and often pinch-hitted for him on speaking engagements. He was literally showered with opportunities to show himself off, and Henry never seemed shy about taking advantage of them. He was a young intellect in a hurry, a schemer, a fellow who enjoyed playing politics, and adored making a big secret out of everything he was up to.

Friends never felt that Henry's life was an open book. There were always little nooks and crannies to it that none of us ever understood."

In his under-graduate years Henry had neither the money or the inclination to wander far from Cambridge. But it was different now. His work with the C.I.A., Army Intelligence and the Seminars shuttled him back and forth between Massachusetts, New York and Washington.

Here again we meet that tantalizing sentence first found in Henry's army career. "He always seemed to know beautiful girls." Testimony for this comes not from his Harvard fellow-students but from the young foreigners who collected annually for the Seminars. As Henry carefully picked and chose those accepted he was also the C.I.A. representative in charge of cultivating them. In short, showing them a good time.

This was duck soup for a young man who had picked up a taste for the good life during his days as a Military "governor" with the U.S. Army of Occupation in Germany. The young intellectuals from abroad wanted mostly to see New York, especially its *sin spots*, Greenwich Village, Harlem, the Broadway district. Henry knew them well, both from experience and heresay. In the pre-war depression days life out on New York town wasn't exactly the bone-crushing financial adventure it is today. Young people knew the tricks of getting through an evening in the Village on a few dollars, and there were always those late night gathering spas, the Automat and all-night cafeterias, where the visitor might enjoy a bird's eye view of the Big Apple's seamy life. You could be sure of running into a pair of hard-bitten whores, a couple of pimps, some worn-out intellectuals, a transvestite or two and a character that could easily be fictionalized into a greasy hood of some neighborhood notoriety. Escorting out-of-towners through New York depended a lot for flavor on the guide's imagination and his capacity for catering to his client's tastes.

Henry, evidently, was quite a master. His little black book produced an endless array of dazzling dolls, Village and Broadway types, who were only too pleased to share the largesse he was able to offer them and his foreign friends. Uncle Sam may be one of the chintziest of employers in many respects, but when it comes to Intelligence the purse strings are inclined to loosen, particularly in areas involving fleshy pleasures.

Recently in dimissing Government charges against two Indian defendants in the Wounded Knee case United States District Judge Fred J. Nichol lashed out at the F.B.I. and expressed incredulity that they would act as they did when two agents squired a prospective witness around Wisconsin last month. He was paid more than two thousand dollars for perjured testimony, said the judge, was housed in a "plush resort," was given all the liquor he wanted and allowed to pick up a call girl at a local bar. "I will say this for the agents, though," said Judge Nichol, "When the witness asked if he could take the girl back to the resort they said no. They said he could take her somewhere else, but not to the resort."

Henry Kissinger's discretion in like situations is not on the record, but one Seminar participant

71

being cultivated as a future source of information for the C.I.A. recalled, "Henry made extravagant promises of the beautiful girls he'd introduce us to and the good times we would have in New York. I have to admit that he was almost right. The women were knockouts and while we didn't hang around the posh East Side boites we did see what we wanted—the Village and Times Square. And we got to visit people's homes. That's something that's always missing when a foreigner goes abroad. Henry certainly wasn't a big spender—no one expected him to be. We were satisfied with the kind of evening he planned for us."

Funds for the Kissinger tours in New York night life came, of course, from the C.I.A. and were funneled into the Seminar's pocket. Henry suffered no more than an occasional hangover. He was a careful drinker, a young man who could hold his own and rarely got to the point where he lost his poise.

Since Henry's social life accelerated only during the weeks when the Seminars were meeting he was able, on campus, to continue the myth of the studious Kissinger, the intellectual totally wrapped up in his work who even forbade Ann to speak to him when he was involved in his ambitious doctoral dissertation. He originally intended writing a trilogy about the century of peace in Europe between 1814-1815 and the outbreak of World War I in 1914. Only the first part was ever completed. It was called *A World Restored: Castlereagh and Metternich, and the Restoration of Peace 1812-1822.*

The massive seven hundred page thesis, meticulously typed by Ann, dealt largely with two unusual diplomats, Lord Castlereagh, the British Foreign Secretary and Prince Metternich, the Austrian political genius.

It focused on the diplomatic efforts of the two men to restore order to Europe after twenty-five years of war and revolution. Wrote Kissiner: "This was the moment when it became evident that Europe was not to be organized by force. What is surprising is not how imperfect was the settlement that emerged, but how sane, not how 'reactionary,' according to the self-righteous doctrines of Nineteenth Century historiography, but how balanced. It may not have fulfilled all the hopes of an idealistic generation, but it gave this generation something perhaps more precious; a period of stability which permitted their hopes to be realized without a major war or a permanent revolution."

In his research for the lofty work, Kissinger could not have overlooked the fact that Clemens Lothar Wenzel Metternich whom he so admired was one helluva Nineteenth Century swinger—the kind of fellow encyclopedias describe as a "licentious man of pleasure."

His escapades were celebrated in one of the all-time movie greats, *Congress Dances*, starring Lillian Harvey and Conrad Veidt, among the last of the fine films Germany was famous for in the pre-Hitler era. It dealt with the Congress of Vienna which lasted nine months, from September, 1814, to June, 1815, and it was the climax of Metternich's work of reconstruction.

He had precise ideas about the basis for a new order in Europe to follow the defeat of Napoleon's ambitions to impose his will on the continent of Europe. Metternich promulgated the idea of creating a "balance of power"—a philosophy that has appealed to Kissinger's pragmatic mind and millions of other people who never made it to Secretary of State.

According to the movie—and to history—Metternich pushed his work forward not only in the conference halls but in the boudoirs of Vienna. He turned on all that city's charm by framing the Congress as a splendid social event. He reduced Elsa Maxwell to the dimensions of a Boise garden club hostess as he arranged a succession of dazzling balls where the orchestra played Viennese waltzes, the wine sparkled and lovely ladies, all looking like beautiful, blonde Lillian Harvey, did their thing—luring heads of state into the bedrooms of Vienna's baroque places while the statesmen did the work.

Metternich, of course, saved a few of the available dolls for himself. He played on women as he did men's minds. As an envoy in the foreign service of Austria he enjoyed a colorful reputation as a diplomat who, when he couldn't win a point from an adversary, simply reached through his wife. The wives of European diplomats supplied Metternich wherever he went with enough information on the affairs of state to render redundant the services of Austrian spies.

Kissinger's admiration for Metternich, respect for Germany's Iron Chancellor, Bismark, and others like them, inspired one Kissinger critic to snarl, "Henry's sincerity is like theirs—a millimeter thick." His choice of doctoral subject dismayed Harvard professors like Carl Friedrich who pointed out that Austrian and British statesmen-aristocrats were "not very much liked figures in academia."

This antagonism to Henry's doctoral work proved extremely valuable later—as the excuse for one glaring gap in Kissinger's Harvard experience. After he received his Ph.D. degree, it was taken for granted that Henry would be promoted from instructor to assistant professor. He wasn't—and that became a dark incident in the Kissinger climb to success never mentioned in his presence. He was proposed for the faculty and there was, to their credit, considerable support among some professors, but enemies blackballed him and he decided to leave the following year.

It took a while for the truth to come out, and when it became known, it amounted to nothing more than the fact that Kissinger had made himself a pretty obnoxious fellow around Harvard. He lacked the kind of emotional pull that might have swayed his enemies into passing over his personality flaws in light of his enormous intellectual capacities and accomplishments.

It was a break actually, for Kissinger had worn his mask of scholar long enough. He had long thought of himself as a political activist, an innovator, not a philosopher-statesman who created ideas and left their accomplishment to the diplomats. For Kissinger the action lay not behind the ivy walls of a college campus but in New York and Washington. He turned down offers of faculty tenure at the University of Chicago and the University of Pennsylvania.

By this time Kissinger had a wide acquaintance in the political world and the charm he never squandered on his classmates was saved for the likes of guest speakers like Arthur Schlesinger, Thornton Wilder, Eleanor Roosevelt, Walter Reuther and William Buckley. Their phone numbers, along with the dolls in the Village, were carefully noted in his little black book.

As Henry quit Harvard and moved to New York and an apartment on East 73rd Street, there was little doubt that he had been deeply hurt by the slight for, after all, his academic qualifications were impeccable. Had it been layered with anti-Semitism? "No," said a faculty member, "And I doubt Henry could ever countenance that explanation. Besides being cordially disliked for his attitudes there was the feeling among more thoughtful faculty members that Henry was too much the opportunist, that he wanted a post on the Harvard faculty only to serve his own interests, to further his private ambitions. They were right, of course, as his career has shown."

Bismark, Kissinger wrote, was a man of many roles and many seasons. "What is an opportunist?" he once was asked. "He is a man who uses the most favorable opportunity to carry through what he regards as useful and appropriate."

PART TWO

"I Spy"

"It took me years to become thoroughly loathed at Harvard. Here in Washington, it happened almost overnight" —Henry Kissinger.

CHAPTER TWO

When you live in Henry Kissinger's fish bowl at Foggy Bottom any number of myths, personal and professional, are bound to spawn. Some are based on fact; others, the pure imagination of their creators. But no one can doubt that his long friendship with Nancy Maginnes provided steadying influence on his mercurial moods.

Nancy and Henry met, they say, sometime in the late fifties. There are gossipists who insist Nancy brought Henry to the attention of her employer, Nelson Rockefeller. She was one of many efficient secretaries working in his office, a handsome woman, six feet tall with bushy, blonde-streaked hair. She is, of course, now Mrs. Henry Kissinger. He stands five feet eight.

Nancy's features are well-drawn but not organized into a classic beauty. There is some hint of sadness in her face, some clue that she has not laughed all her way to the pinnacle of the Washington social ladder. Her hazel-green eyes reflect alertness and interest in everything around her. She's one of those people who want to know how things work. She has the voice and clear diction of a woman who has been in authority a long time. She is thirty-nine, the graduate of a previous marriage to a man older than herself. She remained a bachelor girl for some years afterward. When Nancy met Henry it was, pals maintain, love at first sight—and she obviously was willing to wait.

Nancy has taken becoming a celebrity in stride. She gives a solid newspaper interview and has earned respect for being the wife of a difficult man. She admits being surprised by the super-celebrity status of her husband and longs for more privacy. Henry, she said, "could live without the celebrity part. What he couldn't live without is a job that stimulated him."

The Kissingers are supposed to have met at one of the many functions presided over by the Rocke-fellers. The anecdote which pops up the most frequently places the meeting in the early fifties when Henry attended the same party and started talking to the tall woman for the first time. Their conversation gravitated to Governor Rockefeller.

Kissinger flipped, "Nelson has a second-rate mind, but a first rate intuition about people. Whereas I have a first rate mind and a second rate intuition about people. I have an intuition about you, if you'd care to hear about it."

In Nancy's circles that sort of pitch sounded less awkward than it might elsewhere. She was taken with the portly, bespectacled professorial man with the strange accent and she became one of the women Kissinger was seen with from time to time around town. Kissinger by this time was well enough known to have become a minor celebrity.

The Rockefellers became Henry's newest sponsor after he left Harvard. He had begun to live by the old academic precept, "Publish or perish," and books and articles began to pour from his head as though he imagined himself the Edgar Wallace of the political and intellectual world. Like some writers he had his flops, but one book, *Nuclear Weapons and Foreign Policy*, hit the bull's-eye, becoming a *Book-of-the-Month* selection, selling over seventy thousand hard-cover copies and still going strong in paperback.

The work had begun as a collaborative effort of the Council of Foreign Relations which wanted a public study of the factors involved in the making and implementing foreign policy in the nuclear age. Ultimately, it became a Kissinger solo effort. He shyly took the bows.

Said Kissinger, "I am sure that the book is the most unread best-seller since Toynbee." Kissinger won the Woodrow Wilson Prize and a citation from the Overseas Press Club. *The Washington Post* called it "the most important book of 1957" and it prompted a congratulatory letter from Vice-President Richard Nixon. Secretary of State John Foster Dulles had to read it since Kissinger challenged his viewpoint of "massive retaliation." Kissinger pushed for a new school of thought which discarded World War II notions about "unconditional surrender." He argued that in the New World, with America's nuclear bombs balanced against the Soviet Union's, limited wars for specific political objectives were the only plausible ones.

The Pentagon was horrified by Kissinger's theories and fearful of the book's success—after they read the "dirty part"—which called for a merger of the Army and the Air Force into a single service.

It was the book and Kissinger's work for the Council on Foreign Relations that brought him to Rockefeller's attention. He appointed him director of the Rockefeller Brothers Fund Special Studies Project. Rockefeller was Eisenhower's special assistant to international affairs. Kissinger was invited to serve in a second-echelon job as a foreign policy strategist. He accepted although he was hardly considered a committed Republican. He had nothing to do with Eisenhower, a state of affairs that evidently suited everyone fine.

The Rockefeller salary paid for some more writing and Henry's fame spread. In 1957 he went back to Harvard—this time as a lecturer in government. His course was popular but students found Henry shrill, caustic, sometimes bored. He was impatient of mediocrity—a quality inescapable in a classroom, even at Harvard. Kissinger may have been surprised to discover that he wasn't as fond of teaching as he'd imagined and that the loss of a full professorship hadn't been as great as he thought.

The Eisenhower years, as they were for most people, were quiet, the last peaceful ones Henry Kissinger would see for a long time. The two Kissinger children were born, David and Elizabeth. Ann had always wanted children and Henry could no longer protest that they couldn't afford them. Henry drew income from a wide variety of sources, his appointment, teaching, lectures, book royalties, TV appearances, special assignments in Washington at a hundred dollars a day. While it can be said that Kissinger's years at this period of his life were quiet, it did not necessarily follow that they were idle. Kissinger had always been a man capable of spreading his energies around.

The Kissingers' private life, even with the birth of the children, had dwindled down to a barely supportable relationship. Henry's temper tantrums, friends maintain, became more frequent. The emotionalism that the public saw at Salzburg was anything but new in the life and character of Henry Kissinger. It was not the kind of feeling that could be cut off by a "good night's sleep."

Henry Kissinger's personality has been dissected by experts and inevitably they lean on his Jewish background, his problems as a refugee and the bitterness he must harbor because of those youthful persecutions under Hitler. Overlooked, it would seem, is that Kissinger's character is so typically Bavarian that you expect him at any minute to slip into *lederhosen* and yodel.

When the Austrian journalists muttered facetiously about *Der Foehn* affecting Henry in the famous Salzburg press conference they were only half-kidding. The Alps, the lakes, the rolling countryside, the antiquity of Bavaria, its politics, centuries-old, have gone into the making of numeous men in that province of Germany who look like Henry Kissinger and think like him—even if they aren't as world famous. The Bavarian loves the good life, his wine, his beer, his pipe. He's got wit, humor, and charm. He breathes politics with astonishing fervor and he brawls over politics with the readiness of an Irishman. He's moody, given to dark hours—because of the *Foehn* he likes to believe.

He cries a lot, when he hears the old songs, when he finds a lonely *edelweis*. Give him a few beers and he's an emotional slob—too consumed in his own self-pity to wipe the tears away. He's a romantic—hopelessly in love with love. Good manners are instilled into him from birth. He bows from the waist to women and smiles. There's none of the Prussian arrogance about the gesture. And when he passes a friend on the street he tips his hat and says not *Good Morning* but *Gruess Gott*—the Greetings of God. For a fellow sprung from the soil of farmland his intellect is refined to razor-edge sharpness by centuries of culture that are his heritage. The Bavarian is a complicated man and even to simplify him is to invite the bewilderment so many people find in the personality of Henry Kissinger.

Staying married to Henry for as long as she did could not have been easy for Ann Fleischer and the silence that surrounds those years bear this out. Friends who knew them well in the student days claim the marriage was stormy, fretful, filled with arguments. Others maintain they strolled the streets and parks of Cambridge hand in hand. Holding hands in Bavaria in public carries the same emotional impact as waiting for the signal to change. Everybody does it.

Henry Kissinger, the superman, super-lover,

super-swinger who would enliven the Nixon administration began to grow furtively. The chances are that in the antiseptic world of Nixonites whose crew cuts, manicured nails and Brooks Brothers suits gave one the feeling that they considered sex contemptible, Kissinger would never have stood even a chance at the brass ring if his secret propensity for dolls and dolls had been known. In any event, for years he kept his private life fairly private—which wasn't difficult then for Kissinger wasn't exactly a household word.

There was Nancy, but what could be made of their being seen around together? After all, they worked for the same boss and outside their own circle their private meetings were nobody's business.

Kissinger appeared then to have dug the intellectual type—girls with sorority pins, who were occupying space on Madison Avenue until they found the right stock broker to take them to Scarsdale. Quite a few of this genre found their way onto his arm and for a while there was one lovely young lady who even travelled abroad with him.

But Kissinger appeared to relish the role of the travelling salesman—the young diplomat with a lady diplomat in every town. Just like his hero, Metternich. Whenever he appeared in Paris or the other spots in Europe he was shipped to in the Eisenhower days some shapely beauty always appeared and helped take care of the cold, lonely nights. There weren't too many of these trips abroad though because Nelson Rockefeller liked to have him close to home.

Theirs was the dream match of mind and patron. The little professor yearned for power. The man of wealth had the money to buy it and he was gearing up for a run at the presidency.

Rockefeller's enthusiasm for Kissinger was limitless. "He was a man with ideas," said Rocky, "and he was willing to take the responsibility for organizing them. He understood exactly what I wanted to do. And he could take hold. He knew who to get to write papers, and if he didn't know them he knew how to get the best people in the country."

Rockefeller had taken Kissinger with him into a typical Rockefeller project—a study of America's assets and debits to be mined by the finest minds available. Continued Rocky, "I never was in competition with Henry. Which is very important. I'm not an intellectual. I enjoy talking to intellectuals. I'm constantly trying to draw them out, learn from them, but I'm no competition at all. That relaxed Henry. He could learn what he needed from the environment he was in."

It was an extraordinary environment for a young man of thirty-three with little executive experience. He was confronted with supervising a staff of more than a hundred and, unlike the army, there was no manual to help him. He had to find his own way—It was like being in an alien land again. This was Henry's social introduction to the world of the elite, people he had looked at from afar when he ran the Harvard Seminars. Then, their conversation had been polite, business-like. Now, people like Nelson Rockefeller wanted to know what he thought.

The young man was anything but overwhelmed. David Rockefeller remembered him saying before he joined the family project, "I want to have control over everything I write." Rockefeller added, "He also wanted control over everything else, what subjects would be investigated and who would do the investigating. His self-confidence was awesome."

Rockefeller chose Albany in 1960, leaving the presidential concession speech to John F. Kennedy to Richard Nixon whose heavy beard and artificial personality had lost him the debates with the personable, handsome New Englander.

Like most intellectuals of the era the prospect of the Kennedy Administration filled Kissinger with excitement. The idea of the *New Frontier*, so beautifully articulated in Kennedy's Inaugural Address, stirred hearts and minds that had been depressed by the lacklustre eight years of the Eisenhower Government. America hadn't felt the same twinge of sincere patriotism since Franklin D. Roosevelt started rolling back the Depression in March of 1933 with his words, "We have nothing to fear but fear itself."

Before the Kennedy invasion of Washington the President-elect and Kissinger had met. They admired each other, and Kennedy appreciated Kissinger's writings. He was anxious to abandon the Dulles doctrine of massive retaliation for graduated military response to the Communist challenges. For Kissinger, it was a time of high hopes and he fully believed he was to become an integral part of the news and administration.

It wasn't to be. Kissinger fell into the Kennedy style all right—welcome because of the contrast his very appearance brought to it. The soft-faced intellectual with baggy pants, sharp humor, the rumpled look showed that the Kennedy people were democratic, ready to listen to everybody. Kissinger looked as though he were going to be a big asset. He believed that himself.

He started at the top and slid slowly downhill. The Kennedy people didn't leave him hanging in the breeze. Kissinger got out on his own.

The business to stay out of these days, it seems, is the Presidency. Not quite as steady as it used to be. But the business of being presidential advisor is something else again—as professors, especially from Harvard, have learned. You get on a train early in the morning, carry your briefcase down to Washington, consult with the President if he happens to be there and happens to want to see you and back you go that evening to Cambridge a few hundred dollars richer.

On days when you don't make it in to see the President you can relax in a park or go to a skin flick. Some consulting professors have been known to patronize massage parlors. Sex is a big thing in D.C. in the afternoon—there's so little of it at night when, like the song says, men dance with their wives.

Arthur Schlesinger, Jr. assumed Kissinger's role of patron in the Kennedy court and for some months Henry took weekly trips to Washington, serving as a part-time consultant. But there really wasn't much to consult about Kissinger was against everything that Kennedy supported. The

Berlin Wall disturbed him. Kennedy privately felt it would stabilize the situation in East Europe; publicly, he protested it. Kennedy promulgated the Grand design—expansion of the Common Market into an embryonic European federation. Kissinger felt the President was ignoring the post-war tide of nationalism that was evident in Europe, especially in DeGaulle's France.

Kissinger tried his best to achieve face-to-face meetings with J.F.K. but Kennedy men stood in the way. He got the runaround and, as in rejecting Kissinger for a Harvard professorship, some of the fault lay with Henry's abrasive personality. Kennedy found him overbearing, a "little harassing." Kissinger got the message and quit calling at the White House.

Kissinger, sent to Asia, for a series of minor diplomatic meetings, was asked by reporters if Pakistan would enter into an alliance with China. "No," said Kissinger decisively, "Pakistan would never do anything so foolish." The remark made for most undiplomatic headlines. There were complaints from Pakistan officials to Foggy Bottom about Henry's glib talk—and that about wrote "finish" to his career in the *New Frontier*.

Henry, encouraged to resign, quit in a huff and became surly, pouty, sullen—Bavarian. He complained about the "poor-little-rich-boy" mentality of the Kennedys, he was concerned by the optimism that flooded the White House and the *New Frontier*.

He wanted the Administration to worry about Charles DeGaulle, to reconsider its paternalism toward Europe and he wrote that America should not try to impose its solutions on European problems. "If we insist on remaining the sole trustee of policy everywhere, including Europe, the strain on our resources will be too great. The day will come when we will consider a measure of autonomy in Europe a blessing rather than an irritant."

Several years later, in a less huffy, Bavarian mood, Kissinger conceded, "I first saw government at a high level in the early 1960's . . . . a spirit prevailed which was quintessentially American, that problems are a challenge, not an alibi; that men are measured not only by their success but also by their striving."

Kissinger conceded though that Kennedy's handling of the Cuban Missile Crisis had been masterly, saying, "The administration demonstrated skill, daring and decisiveness." This was high praise from a man whose nose was out of joint, but Kissinger realized his time had not yet come, that playing around with the Kennedy boys was only the warm-up for the years ahead. He still had his patron, Nelson Rockefeller. Their careers remained inexorably linked. And there was another patron standing in the wings—Lyndon Baines Johnson. Henry Kissinger had not quite gotten out of the "presidential advisor" business.

After President John Kennedy lashed out at the steel manufacturers and forced them to roll back steel prices, a group of Wall Street men sat dejected over lunch in their private dining room atop a downtown skyscraper. One shook his head and noted sadly, "It's too bad. We should have elected Kennedy Pope." The others looked at him surprised, "Elected him Pope? Why?" "It's simple," said the first man, "then we'd only have to kiss his ring."

It had been a generation since America had jokes going around like that about the President. And the President they told them about, F.D.R., was the American who laughed loudest.

It was a good thing for the country that Jack Kennedy occupied the White House for the short period he did. There was candor about the man that voters reacted to, the feeling that he was ninety-percent honest, a pretty good average for a Chief Executive. They needed the breather Kennedy provided, the confidence and the jokes, for the shadow was about to fall on the long years of distrust in government without parallel in the history of modern America.

Lyndon Johnson's assumption of the presidency initiated the Dr. Strangelove era, the cover-up, the dealing from the bottom, the manipulation, the new official language found in linguistic horrors like "body count" and while Henry Kissinger did not thrive under L.B.J. the opportunity to serve his third President offered Henry a rare opportunity to sharpen his capacities for spying and his devotion to secrecy. It amounted to a dress rehearsal for Kissinger's star spot with Nixon.

Johnson escalated the Viet Nam War and worried about it. He didn't trust the C.I.A. reports of our progress there. He turned to Ambassador Henry Cabot Lodge whom he had reappointed to Saigon for help. Lodge, a Republican, had been held over from the Kennedy administration in what amounted to an unsubtle attempt to create the atmosphere of bi-partisan support for the controversial war. The only persons convinced that it worked were Johnson and Lodge who, two years earlier, had been adversaries for the vice-presidency.

Lodge recommended Henry Kissinger as a logical man to make a confidential canvass of the situation, even if he was a European specialist, more at home in the West and in involvement with his political passion, nuclear strategy. Lodge, aware of the Kissinger temperament, his abrasive personality and the bitterness of his Kennedy disillusionment, nevertheless felt him the best man for the job. He knew Henry from Harvard, respected his abilities.

Under auspicious auspices—those of the President and Ambassador Lodge—Kissinger undertook his first official trip to Viet Nam. All he knew beforehand was what he had read in the newspapers. He couldn't help but note, however glumly, that the press, appearing better informed than the Administration, took a dim view of White House optimism and unlike the President and his advisors could see "no light at the end of the tunnel"—one of those *Newspeak* crostics being manufactured daily in Washington.

Kissinger's experience with the C.I.A. paid off. Or maybe it was a spy movie. He realized that the most sources of information he would ordinarily meet as an undercover White House operative represented vested interests—military officers, diplomats and business men who generally relayed the kind of information Washington wanted to hear.

So Kissinger decided to stray from the beaten path, to go forth and meet the other Viet Nam outside Saigon, the pleasure palaces and the international intrigue. He talked to everybody—Buddhist leaders, local intellectuals, small business men, farmers, political bosses in the hamlets. He worked like a newspaperman, even spending a half hour in animated conversation with a hundred-and-five year old woman who got angry and tried to choke him. "She was strong," he complained.

When he was through Kissinger knew more than the diplomats, less than the foreign correspondents who had been on the scene for years. With characteristic throughness he had done his homework, covering the logical areas and coming up with logical conclusion, the equivalent of those available in the metropolitan newspapers of any American city. He had achieved a capsule appreciation of Viet Nam, her people, traditions, cultural range, capabilities. In short, Kissinger looked for the answers to the *$64 Questions*—could Viet Nam handle a war and what was the payoff to the United States for the money, troops and machinery we were pouring into it?

On returning to the capital Kissinger's off-the-record answer consisted of a three-word response to, "What's the solution?" He said, "There is none."

On the record, Kissinger stopped at the Rand Corporation Think Tank in Santa Monica, California, and the experts there maintained that Kissinger's reportage gave them the "most brilliant analysis of the war they had ever heard."

Kissinger said, "We are pursuing a very erroneous military strategy, we are fighting not a counter-insurgency operation but a conventional war against a non-conventional enemy. We have nailed our flag to the mast of worthless Saigon politicians and generals. He later wrote: "The war in Viet Nam is dominated by two factors; withdrawal would be disastrous, negotiations are inevitable."

At this point the Kissinger and the press went separate paths. Correspondents could see no future in continuing the action and were all for packing up and coming home—leaving destiny, not men thousands of miles away, to adjust the complexities. But they could find some area of agreement in Kissinger's dismay "at the almost total lack of political maturity or unselfish political motivation among the leaders of the government."

He stopped short of calling the Saigon government a bunch of crooks but he noted the corruption visible even to the undiplomatic eye and felt that Americans were being taken for a ride. But Henry, ever the hard-liner, worried about the possibility of a victory by the North. He said, "A victory by a third-class Communist peasant state would strengthen the most bellicose factions in the internecine Communist struggle around the world."

Kissinger's report impressed President Johnson and, while the Harvard brain wasn't exactly his style, he took the rumpled professor into the fold.

They had little in common beyond their deviousness. And love of mystery.

Kissinger brought his report back to the boss men first, Johnson and Lodge; then, sneaked into Foggy Bottom where he briefed State Department policy makers and fellow spies in small groups—at his suggestion. This became the Kissinger technique—establishing his personal importance and endowing the intimate briefings with an air of secrecy. The Kissinger way was as Bavarian as *apfel strudel*, but the boys at State were impressed and few were aware that a comprehensive account of the Henry Kissinger-Clark Clifford Viet Nam caper had been filed for the *Los Angeles Times* by veteran Far Eastern expert Jack Voise.

Not to worry! L.B.J. took Henry Kissinger on as his personal spy. Both men loved the masquerade as Henry slid in and out of Viet Nam, bringing back secret reports for Johnson's eyes only which were not to be shown to Dean Rusk. The Secretary of State had serious disagreements with Kissinger, and he was one of the reasons for the secrecy cloaking the Harvard man's missions. Grown men in Washington can be awfully childish. Doubtless, Rusk had his own spies tailing Kissinger.

At any rate in his first top drawer Intelligence Job Kissinger became the key man in a mission called Pennsylvania which started the exchange of messages between Washington and Ho Chi Minh. Kissinger stumbled into the secret correspondence through a one-time French resistance fighter, Raymond Aubrec, whom he was introduced to in

Paris. Aubrec was host to Minh when the latter visited Paris in an unsuccessful quest for Viet independence from France in 1946. He spent some time in Aubrec's villa.

Kissinger was forty-three years old when he started playing "I Spy" with Lyndon Johnson. Since the Big Texan was his third President and third big round in Washington, he'd gotten over his pout with the Kennedys, and realized that politics was like a pogo stick. You jump up and down with the springs and you arrive at "up" as often as you reach "down."

There was not much he could give these men, Presidents Eisenhower, Kennedy and Johnson and Nelson Rockefeller too, besides his brains. Their reward to him would be the broadening of his power base. They possessed so much they could afford to throw a little Henry's way.

But there was something else—an intangible— that they all showed chubby Henry Kissinger. They convinced him by their deeds and way of life that he was just like the reducing ads claimed —a skinny, handsome prince wrapped in a chubby package longing to get out—and swing. He had seen their great power first hand and hadn't been impressed. This was the kind of stuff he'd read about in books. It wasn't so easy to come by information on how men of power scored —and come to think of it—it had been a long time since pretty German *frauleins* made his bed and cooked him *leberknoedeln*, because he was *Herr Boss of Belsheim*.

When Henry met Ike, the president was more interested in scoring on the golf course than with WACS. No matter, the good General had a solid sack record to look back on. The general who had the Eisenhower jacket tailored especially for him wasn't out to impress General Patton or to compete with Montgomery's beret. He was middle-aged brass but his slim, trim, waistline wasn't—or the rest of his physical equipment. That was the message the General was sending out—and it worked. Ike got around—and to more places than Normandie.

Poor Ike. His extra-curricular life became top secret in Washington when his name first came to prominence as a potential President. Secretary of State/General of the Armies Marshall and President Harry Truman nipped his affair with a pretty WAC chauffeur and sent Ike back to Mamie and the genial couple landed in the White House, respectable as all get out and homey as an old pair of shoes.

If all the pretty young things who claimed they had spent a quiet half hour or so with Jack Kennedy were laid end to end they'd reduce the Great Wall of China to the size of MacDougall's Alley. Not even a Kennedy could have handled that many, but there were some and in substantial enough numbers to make him the envy of lesser mortals. Kissinger couldn't help but compare himself to the Kennedys no matter how briefly he was exposed to them. He told friends how humiliated and mortified he was in the presence of suave smoothies like the Kennedy brothers, Dean Acheson and others. "They were so witty," Kissinger complained. "He knew he couldn't scintillate like the Jet Set. What invitations he received from them came simply because he was a somebody— an intellectual whose brain power dwarfed everyone else's. Kissinger was a catch at dinner or cocktails—but not for the reasons that Henry wanted to be.

Then he'd seen toothy Nelson Rockefeller at work and at play. He was someone who got around and could say, "how ya cutie" just as persuasively as "hi ya fella." No one ever heard of Happy, Rocky's happy little side kick until there was a fire at the Albany State House. Rockefeller, Mrs. R., the kids, Lieutenant Governor Wilson and the missus—all piled out on the street to watch the firemen put it out. And so did an unannounced house guest—Mrs. Happy Murphy. In the scandal sheets she overnight became famous as the *Mrs. Murphy in Rocky's Chowder*.

That's how it was with the powerful. They had their power—and their fun too. L.B.J. was no exception—even if Lady Bird kept an eagle eye on Lyndon's roving eyes and hands.

Henry Kissinger got the message all right and started to do something about it. This was about the time the Kissingers had reached the conclusion that their marriage was over. Henry and Ann had come far since the days when they drove a second-hand car around Cambridge and lived in a small apartment with made-do furniture and the household was dependent as much on her pay as Henry's teaching income.

They now lived in Belmont Hill, an exclusive neighborhood, could afford help and to send their children to private school. For many couples Henry's prominence, the financial security they enjoyed, the promise of the future would have been the fulfillment of a lifetime of dreaming and planning. For Henry and Ann Kissinger their lives had become an empty shell. Their problem was the old, familiar one of couples who had known each other so long that too soon after marriage each took the other for granted. It was an easy rut for Henry, because of his intellectual curiosity, the wide range of his interests and that success came with comparative ease, few setbacks. What career problems he met were disappointments rather than tragic losses.

Henry quickly outgrew Ann—at least in his mind's eye. He failed to recognize that she was no longer the high school girl he once knew but a lively, intellectual mind, frustrated by Henry's busy life. She was constantly at his beck and call, typing his papers when they were younger, catering to his needs as he floated in and out of their home, often sleeping only four or five hours a night.

Ann was made to feel inadequate—a consort-housekeeper rather than a wife. That's how many marriages ended up in Bavaria. Once Henry made his wife sit outside while he delivered an address in a Washington hotel ball room. When he was talking with friends of an evening he often told her get lost. He showed no interest in the children, leaving their upbringing and care totally in Ann's hands.

The children, until they reached an age where he could talk to them, made Kissinger nervous,

© Lorillard 1975

If you have
a taste for quality,
you'll like the taste
of Kent.

King Size
or Deluxe 100's.

Kings: 16 mg. "tar," 1.0 mg.
nicotine; 100's: 18 mg. "tar,"
1.2 mg. nicotine av. per cigarette,
FTC Report Oct. '74.

Newport

Alive with pleasure!

Newport

20
CLASS A
CIGARETTES

Newport

MENTHOL KINGS

18 mg. "tar", 1.2 mg. nicotine, av. per cigarette, FTC Report Oct. '74.

neighbors said. One recalled, "I never saw him out walking with them. I remember after the breakup he would come in his very fancy Mercedes, to pick up the kids after a long absence and once he said, 'Oh, look what I've done for you children. I've had the car washed.' It was heartbreaking."

Kissinger went to Europe in 1963 with Nelson Rockefeller and abroad came the decision to make a break with Ann. It happened in steps. First he moved to another part of the house. Then he moved out completely and into a fashionable apartment in Cambridge. The separation lasted for a year until Ann, hoping it was only a temporary aberration, broke down and consulted a divorce lawyer.

She went to Reno and in the uncontested divorce was awarded the house and an undisclosed settlement. She sold the house and moved to a smaller place. The divorce papers were sealed and a relative said, "There was no third party involved. Just two people who could no longer live together." Some of his colleagues blamed the various redheads and blondes Kissinger was found with from time to time—and more frequently right out in the open. A woman friend of Henry's said straightforwardly, "It was stifling with Ann. She was totally out of contact with Henry's world —just a simple wife and a good mother. He needed more in a woman than that. You could see him growing more frantic about his private life with each passing year. The miracle was that it lasted so long."

Once Ann started the divorce, Henry began to

blossom out and the giddy shadow of the playboy of the next administration began to be cast around town and in the capitals of Europe. Henry slimmed down and somewhere must have picked up the advice of that perennial womanizer, Al Jolson. "Always wear a tan, kid. You can't go wrong with the fillies." Henry bought himself a sun lamp and the metamorphosis started in earnest.

"Henry was going to London," said Professor Thomas Schelling, "and a friend of mine who was to meet him asked me how he would know him. I said, " 'Oh, a dumpy little fat man will get off the airplane. He will be pale, clumsy, sickish, fif- tyish.' " The man at the airport didn't recognize Kissinger. He'd lost twenty pounds and with that sun lamp complexion even Al Jolson would have been proud of him. And Jolson hated everybody.

Henry underwent an enormous personality change—as though he were secretly taking courses at a Charm School. From a very gruffy, cranky man he had become cheerful—even funny. The quips that used to be lost because they were heard in a sort of Tarzan-like grunt were now polished like jewels and tumbled fast from his lips as though they'd been carefully rehearsed.

The new Henry Kissinger, face it, made quite an impression. Fellow professors marvelled—and with real envy. "You could never make Henry Kissinger into a handsome Casanova, but it would be difficult not to improve him. He had no place to go but up. And I must say he did a splendid job of it after his divorce. He spruced up—looked his age when before he seemed more like his own grandfather. He looked like what he was—a middle-aged professor. When you put that together with his reputation as an intellect you were bound to create a personality that would attract certain women. His work alone made him a catch. Everyone in Washington was aware he was some sort of spy. You couldn't look like Henry did and get away with it unless you had money or were interesting. Washington is that way, you know."

Like John Foster Dulles, Eleanor Roosevelt, Phineas Fogg, Superman and other peripatetic immortals, Henry Kissinger began manifesting himself here, there and everywhere—especially at cocktail parties. The once sullen, grumpy, difficult-to-know intellectual who had given the impression that he preferred balancing books to booze, seemed hopelessly enamored of his new image, the *bon vivant* who revelled in being part of the scene. Gone was the ponderous pedagogue. Hail Kibitzer Kissinger, the Playboy of the Potomac, the Satyr of Sutton Place.

Washington's political merry-go-round and New York's cafe society no longer overwhelmed Henry and vice versa. The teensy-weensy chorine who wouldn't dared to have accosted the awesome Doctor of Philosophy a few or so earlier now found him irresistible. Henry learned to summon her into his orbit with warm, come-hither smiles and suave continental charm. Prince Metternich had nothing on him—despite all that Viennese *schmaltz*. This round-faced fellow had Bavarian *Suesslichkeit (sweetness)*. Kissinger could discuss Dry Manhattan cherries with as much perspicacity as nuclear energy.

Nancy Maginnes had a lot to do with the creation of the new Henry. She attended to the important details of his "coming out"—seeing that he paid more attention to his clothes and urging him to matching socks. Henry was more than docile—anything but the reluctant debutante. He thrived in the giddy climate of the cocktail set and learned to laugh as heartily at the *non sequitur* as Archie Bunker. There hadn't been anyone so cuddly on the free-loaders' circuit since the days of the great Hollywood musicals and S.Z. "Cuddles" Sakall.

Etched into the cornerstone of cafe society was one of the founders, Claire Booth Luce, an all-time champion among the hostesses vying with one another for celebrity guests. An invitation to a Luce affair was a command performance, and the man who snubbed the blonde dynamo risked the wrath of the vast Henry Luce publishing dynasty. Henry, in 1966, had gone to that great publishing executive suite in the sky, and Henry's widow observed the traditional period of mourning and retirement from worldly activity. When it was over her friends prevailed upon Claire to throw a bash —a sort of "coming out" party to signify the end of her sorrow and re-emergence into the social world. Someone suggested, "Why not invite Henry Kissinger?" Claire protested uncharacteristically, "Why, I don't even know him."

The remark fell upon silence, being totally unexpected from the source. When Claire started up the ladder to literary and marital success, she had the reputation of a young, sexy iron butterfly, calculating, ambitious, shrewd. A lady who knew that the route to the top lay in the importance of her connections and no surer ticket existed than firstname friendships with celebrities.

As a young sub-editor on women's magazines Claire's cool-as-a-cucumber technique was to call a Ruth Chatterton, for example, and say that she had just spoken to a Maurice Chevalier who suggested she invite Ruth to a Saturday night buffet for two hundred of his most intimate friends. Even if a Ruth Chatterton recognized the ploy she accepted rather than risk a Chevalier's disapproval. With a Chatterton in the bag, Claire could parlay her into a Chevalier and maybe pick up a Tullio Carmenatti or a Dolly Sister—they went anywhere.

"Claire was absolutely ruthless," remembered a one-time-co-worker. "There were no limits to her ambitions for Claire Booth and no rules she wouldn't break to get where she wanted to be. People were puppets to her, and her whole career is an example of how cleverly she manipulated their strings."

Her post-mourning affair turned out to be a rousing success. It could be no other way, for Claire's talents as a hostess were unsurpassed. As always the centerpiece, stunning in her flowing cocktail gown, beautifully coiffed hair, supple figure, carefully made-up face, it didn't matter that everyone knew she was well into her sixties. Claire Booth Luce transcended age—so long as she remained vibrant, alert and interesting as a woman.

Kissinger had accepted with alacrity; as a matter of fact his R.S.V.P. arrived in the very first batch. Besides knowing better than to refuse, Henry realized important things could happen at Madame Luce's. They often did, and Henry's own experience was to prove that the rule held true. For one of the very special guests Mrs. Luce had invited for that 1967 Christmas gala was someone she admired tremendously, Richard M. Nixon.

Mr. Nixon, a person of no fixed address, was, for the moment, occupying posh digs on Fifth Avenue, hard by the compound of Governor Nelson Rockefeller, Henry Kissinger's sometime boss. He had migrated from California after his ignominious defeat for the governorship of that state by a local politician, Pat Brown and had written a typical Nixon epitaph, "You won't have Dick Nixon to kick around any more" when he told the press he was retiring from politics. No one believed him.

So Dickie became the *Barefoot Boy of Wall Street*, the California kid out of Whittier College and the Navy and the Vice-Presidency who took a hundred thousand dollar a year job with a prestigious Wall Street law firm where he was expected to perform little more than public relations assignments for their prestigious big business clients.

Nixon rode down to the Street in an air-conditioned, chauffeuered limousine when he wasn't out on the road and listening to those who urged him to make another bid for the Presidency. Nixon carefully nudged them to the point where his political future became a conversational topic. He could never be accused of shyness.

Nixon carefully avoided trespassing on Rockefeller's political bailiwick, New York State, and the territory of the mayor, New York City. Nixon was so apolitical that no one outside of the chosen few who worked with him ever really realized he was there. Nixon enjoyed all the benefits of the great city but never found time to apply his expertise in government to any of its problems—even non-political conditions like drug addiction, crime in the streets, the flight of the middle class to the suburbs, the loss of businesses that plagued the Big Town. No one ever heard of Pat Nixon joining the ladies in programs to clean up Central Park, her across-the-street neighbor or even to support the Children's Zoo. Every New York woman of prominence got involved in that.

The Nixons preferred being non-residents so we never knew what an expert Nixon was on big city problems until he hit the stump as a presidential candidate. Then, it was clear why. He'd been studying, doing his homework. From his slick apartment house he looked across Central Park to the slums of the West Side, north to Harlem, south to the troubled worlds of the garment district, Wall Street, Broadway, East to the racial tensions of the Bronx, the dismay of suburbia in Long Island. The solution to everything, he decided, lay in getting urban activist Richard Nixon into the White House.

After Mrs. Luce introduced Kissinger and Nixon they went off to a corner by themselves and talked for about an hour. For Henry, at least, it turned out to be the most rewarding hour of his career.

"It took me years to get thoroughly loathed at

Harvard. Here in Washington it happened almost overnight," Henry Kissinger once said with a touch of sadness behind the sarcasm.

The professor was forty-five in 1968, and for him it was a "do or die" year. In this respect he wasn't alone. His boss, Nelson Rockefeller, was ready to lay millions on the line to grab the prize that had been eluding him for years, the Republican presidential nomination. It was going to be a bruising political year.

For Kissinger it was particularly crucial. He was at a cross-roads. A friend explained, "Henry had tidied up his personal life. He had switched personality and socially, at least, some of the abrasiveness had gone. Hostesses adored his new veneer of Bavarian *suesslichkeit* and he was plainly enjoying fresh kicks from being a roly-poly Casanova. The svelte Henry Kissinger didn't last long. He soon regained his former weight and like most men inclined to portliness he embarked on a succession of diets that persist to this day.

Henry had gained the ear of three Presidents, but never their complete confidence. That was what he wanted, even more than the financial security and the emoluments of being what Sergeant Kraemer had once described as a "phenomenon." On the lecture circuit he could command twelve hundred dollars a night at any time and for whatever number of lectures he chose to give. He was welcome at any university in the world as a guest lecturer but finally achieving a full professorship hadn't fulfilled Henry's ambitions. He had outgrown teaching. Harvard had been correct in rejecting him for tenure back in the fifties—he either subconsciously or cynically saw the academic life as a stepping-stone to what he really sought— a wide, policy making role in world affairs. Kissinger was one of those people, like Nixon, who believed they were divinely ordained to run the universe. Except for the accident of his birth Henry would have set his heart on the presidency.

That he constitutionally was unable to achieve his ambition may have accounted for some of Kissinger's abrasiveness. It haunted him whenever he stepped out of his ivory tower, first, in the academic world; second, in the political arena. A woman staff assistant at Harvard when Kissinger returned there recalled, "His behavior wasn't uniform. He appeared to have this fear that other lecturers were laughing behind his back. I feel certain that if a proper mental diagnosis had been made in 1962, he would have been declared sick. Henry was extraordinarily mercurial in his moods —laughing and joking one minute, nasty the next. He seemed tragically insecure."

Henry's search for security and admiration had often eluded him. The public watched him throw a temper tantrum at Salzburg, but the display was old hat to associates. When he wrote speeches for Rockefeller, campaign workers always said, "Ask Henry about this, even if we've already made up our minds. We don't want to hurt his feelings."

The Kissinger attitude, again, was typically Bavarian. The Bavarian is low man on the totem pole in Germany, the farmer, the peasant, the very word *Bayern* (Bavaria) stems from the noun *Bauer* (peasant), so the need for approval is constant and nagging. Especially when it comes to intellect.

Even Bavarian pedagogues lapse into their dialect and easy-going charming, un-Germanic ways, yet they will turn around suddenly and do something razor-sharp and offensive. They need to prove themselves as Prussian as the North German when it comes to asserting prerogatives of station.

When the Kissingers moved into Belmont Hill, Henry built himself a study. The major irritant was the outside stairway to the office which was situated on top of his garage. "Nice people, if they build an outside staircase on a garage," said a neighbor, "discuss it with their neighbors. It was just a matter of taste." She continued, "I won't say Mr. Kissinger made enemies around here, but the feeling was, 'Who does he think he is?' "

There was a typical Kissinger feud with Professor Robert Bowie, dirertor of Harvard's Center for International Affairs. When Kissinger was associate director, the two men never spoke yet they shared the same phone system. Each had the feeling that he was being overwhelmed by the other.

Although he was a prodigious writer and an influential one, Kissinger never enjoyed the praise he felt his due from other typewriter tappers. "His style has its own carefully plotted symmetry," said one professor, "but it strikes me as being a triumph of stamina over grace." Flipped another, "How a man who is unable to write will write so much and how by iron discipline make it at least half readable is one of Henry Kissinger's outstanding characteristics." Dogged determination to make good and out-fox his detractors appears to have been a burning Kissinger trait. It was as though he bent his whole career toward arriving at the point where he could say, "Well, here I am. I made it. And I did it without any help from anyone."

This, of course, was not true of Henry Kissinger and is less correct now than ever. Kissinger has been led every inch of the way by strong, wealthy, important men who needed him. Without them, there would never have been a Henry Kissinger as head of the State Department. Yet without Kissinger, Rockefeller, Eisenhower, Kennedy, Johnson and Nixon would have followed exactly the same life patterns. It was not a question of one hand washing the other.

Among the more shameful episodes in political history will have to be Nelson Rockefeller's tacit support of Richard Nixon during the scandal-marked two years of his second administration. Time and time again the press and liberal voices in his own party turned to Rocky for some clue indicating the feelings of a man who, everyone knew, had entered the 1968 campaign belatedly in a mini-Stop Nixon movement.

It came too late to work—even if it would have gotten off the ground in the first place. But, at least, Rockefeller showed himself to possess some integrity and was more than a rich man fooling around in politics, lighting up the image of the Rockefeller's international fortune and manipulations. It was the plucky Rockefeller who stood on the convention podium four years earlier and insisted on being heard over the catcalls and jeers of the Goldwaterites.

"Rocky's silence will come home to roost," said one knowledgeable New York Republican, "when he tries for the nomination in 1976. There's going to be a terrific surge toward new faces, and the only way Rocky could ever have masked his old face was by resuming what he once was—his posture as leader of the liberal block of the party."

In the Rockefeller campaign of 1968, Henry Kissinger enjoyed his first flush of the excitement of politics—something that had stirred him before but never reached a boiling point. Now it filled him with excitement.

Henry was right there with the campaign party —travelling with Rocky, his supporters and Nancy Maginnes. They needed Henry—and he knew it and loved it.

Kissinger, like his boss, was worried by Richard Nixon. He didn't want to see him in the White House. "That man is unfit to be President. I would never work for that man. He is a disaster."

So Henry hit the trail with Rocky. Today they say he would prefer to be called "Mr." or "Mr. Secretary" to Doctor Kissinger. It could be, but that wasn't always so. The Rocky people, who cordially dislike his petulance, his need to be smothered with admiration and who really hadn't time to baby him, deliberately introduced Kissinger around as "Mr.". It annoyed him.

Kissinger was reverting to his Bavarian heritage. A title is a title is a title—make no mistake. And the man who doesn't use it, especially if it has been earned, is a rare Bavarian indeed. Hereditary titles flourish to a greater degree only in Spain and Italy where they still carry some legal and political weight. The last Crown Prince of Bavaria was buried in the early thirties at an advanced age of seventy-odd, but his relatives and everyone remotely connected with the Royal Family still cling to whatever honor their names carry, and the number of *Herr Grafs* and *Herr Barons* floating around the countryside would fill a couple of good-sized stadiums. Besides royal titles, there are occupational ones—like Herr Direktor, Herr Beobachter, Herr Inspektor, etc. The title is another manifestation of the Bavarian's search for respect in the German sun.

Henry had tasted the limelight and was still digesting it in the salons of scintillating hostesses like Claire Booth Luce. Now he wanted more. He expected the public at large to become aware of him. So he pushed himself into photographs, trying his best to nudge closer to Rocky. Kissinger seldom made it. Other campaign workers systematically nudged him out. They bumped him from planes, made it tough for him to get transportation at airports. Henry was snubbed right and left during those final few weeks of politicking by the Rockefeller people before Miami.

"It was a bruising experience but, for once, Henry took it with some grace," said a friend. "He charged it up to experience, evidently deciding, with that pragmatic mind of his, that since he'd chosen politics as his life work he might as well become accustomed to the grubby side of it."

"He had so much going for him he could afford to simmer down and play it cool," said a Rockefeller strategist. "His situation papers were brilliant and they were used, every clumsy compound noun and comma of them. He spent a lot brainpower, and Rocky recognized it. Rockefeller didn't carry the weight to win the nomination but his position—basically Kissinger's—was incorporated into the platform."

A Kissinger proposal that did not make it to the platform, of course, lay hidden away in one of Rockefeller's foreign policy speeches and went virtually unnoticed. It was Rocky's promise that, as President, he would visit Red China.

At the Miami convention, Henry Kissinger became one of the most outspoken and articulate voices against Nixon. He warned of the man's dangers intellectually and personally. It didn't take Henry long to master the politician's lingo. He could work both sides of the fence, switching from "sweet nothings" to lashing attack.

Henry's behavior at Miami is all water under the bridge now and, of course, it was conveniently swept under the carpet when he joined the Nixon administration. And the man himself, when he was riding high in the White House, liked to protest that he hadn't been all that tough on the President. But his and Rocky's fears were realistic and their unguarded statements to delegates were sharp and filled with foreboding.

But the complexion of politics changes with dramatic suddenness. When both Nixon and Rockefeller realized their continued sparring might conceivably lead to the nomination of Ronald Reagan who, like Goldwater, saw a military solution as the only logical end to the Viet Nam folly, they bedded down, worked out a platform they could both accept. It was agreed that Rockefeller would retreat gracefully.

It has been said that Richard Nixon always planned one step ahead. During the primaries he planned for the convention. During the convention he planned for the campaign. During the campaign he planned for the Administration—or so it seemed when he sent former Pennsylvania Governor William Scranton winging on a three-week fact-finding tour of Western Europe in mid-campaign.

Yet, after the election, as Nixon shuttled between his interim headquarters at New York's Pierre Hotel, a block from his Fifth Avenue apartment and his bayside cottage at Key Biscayne, he suddenly realized he had made few preparations to staff the Administration.

According to Defense Secretary Clark Clifford, the acknowledged expert on Presidential transitions, there were two thousand plus top-level jobs in the federal government that had to be filled by —or shortly after—Inauguration Day. Among the methods Nixon used to recruit people was to circularize those listed in *Who's Who*—all 66,000 of them—asking for names.

This was how Paul Hoffman described the Nixon "mastery" of the art of government in his excellent book *The New Nixon—a Critical and Skeptical Analysis*.

Nixon, Hoffman wrote, had no problem with his immediate staff and if he had plans for the top White House jobs they seemed to reflect unsuspected generosity and conciliation—for Nixon.

It sounded great on paper—and the way Nixon described it. He was not going to form a coalition government—but it would be the nearest thing to it—ever. Except that it never came off the drawing board.

Hubert Humphrey turned down the ambassadorship to the UN. So did Eugene McCarthy; so did Sargent Shriver. Clifford was sounded out for Defense but he refused to stay on. Nixon tried once more to get a name Democrat in the Cabinet to fulfill the tradition of national solidarity. Henry "Scoop" Jackson wanted to be sure a Democrat would succeed him as the senator from Washington before he would accept the Defense Department. Governor Dan Evans refused.

President-elect Nixon found the going just as tough on the Republican side. Nelson Rockefeller vetoed the UN, his brother, David Rockefeller, rejected Treasury. Massachusetts Senator Edward Brooke turned down Housing and Urban Development. Feelers even went to Thomas E. Dewey who had been out of government and politics for nearly twenty years.

Finally Nixon announced his "team," men without previous experience, names no one would remember with the exception of a couple like Attorney General John Mitchell and Interior Secretary Walter J. Hickel. They would be remembered for different reasons—Mitchell, for his surliness; Hickel, for his guts in calling the turn on the Nixon White House so early in the game.

Explained Paul Hoffman, "Nixon announced the Cabinet *en bloc* in a nation-wide TV special from Washington's Shoreham Hotel. Before presenting the men who would guide the country through the next four years he named Walter Washington as 'Mayor of Washington, D.C.', which impressed critics as a cynical plot to get a black face on TV.

"For the new Cabinet contained no Negro, nor did it include a Jew, a Democrat, nor even a representative of the GOP's liberal wing. It was essentially a slice of Middle America, a bland assemblage of middle-aged management men from business, politics and education."

For Secretary of State, Nixon was forced to pick William F. Rogers, fifty-five, his closest friend in Washington for years, senior partner in one of New York's biggest firms, a man who had compiled a creditable record as Attorney-General, but wholly without experience in foreign policy.

But that was one appointment that didn't worry Richard Nixon in the least. The amateur football coach had long since found his backstop and Henry Kissinger was at his side at the Inauguration on January 20, 1969, a round-faced, owlish, rumpled little man whose name would be the first "household word" of the new administration.

It is Claire Booth Luce who takes full credit for the blooming of Henry Kissinger and Richard Nixon. "It was my idea. I knew that Henry was not a Nixon man, that he didn't like or trust him. But I thought they would hit it off. I told Nixon, 'I think you'll admire Henry.'"

That doesn't jibe with the facts, but it doesn't really matter. Surely when Mrs. Luce found out that the two men were balancing cocktail glasses in her own apartment at a Christmas party she realized they should meet.

The first meeting never warmed up, as Kissinger recalled it some months later. "Neither of us is very good at cocktail-party conversation." That doesn't jibe either with Henry's capacity for developing the *bon mot* into a fine art. But that, one can suppose, depended on the company. Richard Nixon wasn't the kind of man who invited jokes.

Kissinger's impression of the presidential aspirant softened after that meeting. He had met him with all the prejudices of the academic world but found him gentler and "more thoughtful" than he expected.

As for Nixon he knew the professor's work from *Nuclear Weapons and Foreign Policy* which he admired and he respected a Harvard intellectual who stood up against the Bundys and Schlesingers of the Eastern Establishment.

Kissinger's first foray into politics on the convention level had proved enormously rewarding—notwithstanding the slights of being shunted aside when the photographers appeared or being bumped from plane rides. After it was over and the convention bunting packed away, Kissinger's mind and not his photograph was very much in demand. Throughout the Nixon campaign there was a steady stream of calls from his aides. There was John Mitchell, for instance, who called for Kissinger's opinion about the Viet Nam negotiations in Paris.

Other Nixon staffers constantly sought him out

116

and even the Democrats representing Henry Kissinger didn't hesitate to ask his opinion about one aspect of foreign policy or another. It was flattering to be so highly regarded in both camps of the American political scene.

Kissinger privately likes to think himself as an "independent" rather than a member of either party, and this attitude seemed to have paid off. Normally, the independent label is the kiss of death to any politician, even to one like Kissinger who was involved in the non-partisan field of foreign policy. But, then, was Henry really a politician at the time?

He hadn't quite made up his mind. The convention had been great and broadening, but Kissinger was about ready to hit the lecture circuit and the legend goes that he was just leaving for an appointment with the concert booking agent when a call came from Nixon's Pierre Hotel suite saying the President-elect was anxious to meet him.

This had to have startled Kissinger, for a meeting at that time could have only one significance, an invitation to participate in the Government— possibly as a spy, a secret courier or just some extra piece of brainpower Nixon needed to sneak in the back door. It was an odd invitation to a professor who, after the election, had spoken at the Naval War College in Newport, Rhode Island. At luncheon, when the discussion got to the campaign Kissinger described Nixon as "paranoic" and speculated about whether he would be able to withstand the pressures of the White House.

Daniel Ellsberg, of Pentagon papers fame, and no great friend of Kissinger, who has often claimed Henry swiped many of his ideas, confessed surprise at the extent to which Kissinger went in the post-election period to downgrade Nixon. Said Ellsberg, "Everyone was quite amazed that a man connected with these political people would be so frank about the man who had just been elected."

Kissinger would spin his own tales of what he'd said and not said about Nixon before going to work for him. He decided that he'd forgotten everything—which didn't make sense in view of the fame of his powers of retention. Said Kissinger, "My dominant recollection of my feelings about the President was that I didn't think he was fit, that he made me uneasy, and I didn't know anything good about him and I believed the bad things. But I had no independent knowledge. I hadn't ever really seen him before."

Machiavelli said, "The first impression of a ruler and of his brains comes from seeing the men around him." Nixon, who considered carefully his public image, knew that he was in trouble with the selection of Rogers as Secretary of State. He had picked someone whose only real value lay in that he'd keep quiet, be loyal and do what he was told. For a powerhouse, Nixon would have to rely on someone closer to home, a personal advisor to bolster his own high opinion of his expertise in foreign affairs. Nixon had seen enough presidents to realize that most preferred running foreign affairs from the White House at one point or another in their administrations. He would start the policy at the beginning.

"Besides, he was desperate, and he realized that

the appointment of Kissinger would at least show that he had enough brains to recognize intellect," said one White House staffer after Henry had been appointed as an Advisor on Foreign Affairs, a Special Assistant to the President.

Neither man hurried the acceptance although Nixon wanted a hot line installed between them at the outset. Kissinger demurred since he needed to talk to a number of people about the appointment possibility. Teaming up with Nixon might be throwing a curve into his aspirations for the future. After all, he belonged to the opponent's camp and what would they think about a marriage with Nixon?

Rockefeller endorsed it promptly saying, "You've got the opportunity of a lifetime. This man's interest in foreign affairs and our positions are not too far apart." Recalling the pep talk to his protege, Rockefeller said, "I told Henry he had a responsibility. He had spent a lifetime working on these problems. I said I'd do anything I could to support him."

So Kissinger became the most unlikely member of the "German trio" as the three top Nixon aides came to be called. The others were H.R. "Bob" Haldeman, out of advertising, and John Ehrlichman whose ties with Nixon dated back to school days and a period when they were fellow Eagle Scouts. Intellectually neither man could hold a candle to Kissinger—and it was at this point that the difference in their life style began and continued right on down the list to their appearance. Their clothes and hair cut, circa Brooks Brothers and the Main Street Barber Shop, endowed Henry

Kissinger with the most appealing look of his career. He gave the impression of being a cuddly kewpie-doll. Chalk up one score for the Nixon administration.

Kissinger's appointment made him heady news for the first time in his life. It was exciting and pictures of the event show an exhilarated, smiling Henry Kissinger, a fellow who had capped a brilliant career, packed with luck, packed with disappointments, many moments of happiness and some of personal sorrow, standing beside the President of the United States when he said that his orders to Kissinger were to do away with crisis diplomacy, that Kissinger intended to achieve a position in which the United States would be able to do more than just react to events.

"I am one who likes to get a broad range of views expressed," Nixon added, "Dr. Kissinger has set up what I believe is a very exciting new procedure for seeing to it that the President of the United States does not hear just what he wants to hear, which is always a temptation for White House staffers."

If Richard Nixon needed Henry Kissinger desperately for his intellectual savvy, the administration certainly needed someone with his bounce and verve to offset the antiseptic quality that took over the White House when the Nixons moved in. "You know," said one old school politician, "I could smell the *Bon Ami* when I entered the front door. This wasn't the White House I knew but a freshly scrubbed men's john in one of those new

Washington hotels."

Then there's Michael, a wild, irrepressible young lawyer of Irish descent who boasts, "I'm the only bright young lawyer in town on the day they needed a Catholic over there who said 'frig it.' And I've laughed all the way to the poorhouse. Those Katzenjammer Kids, Ehrlichman and Haldeman, scared me right out of the job. They had prejudices I never heard of and when stories began leaking out how they ran the shop I pulled out my rosary and said a decade of *Hail Marys* in gratitude for the wisdom that kept me out of there. They called Haldeman's office the *Berlin Wall*. I used to dream of showing up there one morning in drag and announce that I really was a secret transvestite. Anything to shake them out of their high style, hypocritical torpor. How a fellow like Henry Kissinger stood it I never could rationalize. He must have been a terribly ambitious man.

"There was nothing about him or his life to prepare him for what he was going to meet at the White House. That swinger stuff is just newspaper talk. In his private life he was just a normal man who happened to be divorced and liked the good life—drinking, a beautiful girl, conversation when he could find it, some way to relax. But whoever heard of relaxing at that place? They were on the job sixteen hours a day, and there were more hot lines connected in the District in the first six months of Nixon than there had been in all the years of Johnson. And that's saying a lot. Johnson didn't have an acute case of telephoncitis. His was pathological.

"But there was Kissinger—like a benign Buddha, trying to hide the frantic nerves inside him. He was off and running from the day he stepped in. He thrived on the adversity. With Haldeman and Ehrlichman to stir his contempt I doubt that he would have been as good on the job as he was. He needs to feel challenged, admired, put upon, despised and loved, so he can outperform everyone else. He could have everything he wanted at the White House—except love. Unless Nixon loved him during those last weeks.

"But Kissinger doesn't love people back. So it didn't matter to him. That's what made the difference."

It was almost a year before Henry escaped from the celibacy enforced on him by the Katzenjammer Kids, President Nixon and the real fact that the country had a war on its hands, and his job was extricating America from what daily was becoming a more worrisome dilemma. There was no opportunity to unwind and recreation appeared to be frowned upon inside the White House. The staff grabbed bites to eat when they could. There were long hours spent in the Situation Room and there was nothing of the "easy does it" atmosphere of the Kennedy or Johnson Administrations. Nixon went strictly by the book—his own book. "The Germans didn't have to bow as he walked through the halls," said one ex-White House aide, "but he would have preferred that they did."

Whether Kissinger was a free spirit at heart was severely tested during the first year when the only thing gossip columnists could find out about his private life was that he liked marzipan and canned fish. Kissinger had buried himself in his work and appeared to thrive on the power it gave him. He was like a kid playing with a new toy—and Nixon himself became part of the game. Early in their association, Kissinger realized Nixon was feeding on his intellect. Nixon was like a man hypnotized when Henry was invited to explain his views. A man with so few original ideas of his own, Nixon was totally susceptible to the German's blandishments.

The Kissinger power showed. Reporters got fed up with the canned statements from the State Department and looked to Henry to fill them in on off-the-record situations. Henry tried to cultivate a good press. He didn't know how to handle his people though. They complained and bitched. Kissinger's staff of a hundred had a larger attrition figure than any other White House department.

He got to be known as The Monster—the Dr. Strangelove who mixed mysterious brews, fed them to the President and turned an already devious nature into some sort of evil spirit—not unlike Doctor Kissinger himself. The rumors were wild—and the people outside the White House which already had begun to reflect the zealous protection of its custodians, Haldeman and Ehrlichman, wanted to know more about the government's mysterious alchemist.

It wasn't Nancy Maginnes who finally broke down the castlemoat behind which Henry had been imprisoned but the irresistible combination of Barbara Howar, Gloria Steinem and Sally Quinn.

Barbara Howar had been around Washington most of her adult life and knew the place like a book. She had figured quite prominently in the gay goings-on during the Johnson administration and was the young social secretary lady who confessed that L.B.J. often held her hand while he watched the movies, and just as often fell asleep in the act. Lady Bird bothered to wake him up now and then but didn't seem to be too perturbed, feeling fairly sure that his attentions to Barbara would not reach beyond hand-holding.

Miss Steinem, of course, is the mystique behind some offshoots of Women's Lib, a lady of enormous interests and, like Kissinger, with power. Barbara had decided to give a party for Gloria and invited Sally Quinn, then a *Washington Post* reporter who wasn't even dreaming about becoming the television personality she didn't become. Sally was content then with her role as a solid, fact-digging newspaperwoman. Seeing Kissinger at a cocktail party was, in the parlance of her trade, an "item" and she went to work on it.

Henry, it appeared, was rather sorry he had come. He knew he had developed into a Washington legend as a White House mystery man, but even in Washington people don't barge over and gush, "Oh, you great big Mystery Man. Tell me all about yourself." So Kissinger hid out in a corner, sipping a cocktail while his companion for dinner later that evening, Miss Steinem, did her guest-of-honor duties, meeting all the guests and chatting with them for appropriate periods—the amount of time determined by their official status rather than personality. That is *de rigueur* in D.C.

and Gloria often goes by the rules.

Sally, recognizing Henry, sought him out and, after they talked briefly, she teased him, "You really are a swinger underneath it all, aren't you?"

"Well," Kissinger replied, "you couldn't call me a swinger because of my job. Why don't you just assume that I'm a secret swinger."

The remark went into the history books—along with *My Country Right Or Wrong, Don't Shoot Until You See The Whites of Their Eyes, Shoot This Old Grey Head Instead* and *Bring Us Together*.

Sally Quinn quoted on—and Henry Kissinger's Washington world would never be the same thereafter. With one mighty stroke of the verbal sword he had told Haldeman, Ehrlichman and even President Nixon to go fly a kite. He had extricated himself from the Situation Room and was going to the bedroom and other places where situations were more fun.

They took pictures of Henry and *les girls*—Kissinger with Gloria, Barbara and Sally. From Dr. Strangelove, Henry began his transformation to what Barbara Walters would one day call "The Jackie Onassis of the Nixon administration."

And that was the kind of person the Nixon administration needed—a Jackie Onassis even if she came in male clothing. Washington was badly in need of someone to talk about. Gossip had about gone out of style until Secret Swinger Kissinger got into the act and put it back into its proper perspective—as a capital staple that belonged with hors d'oeuvres, champagne, the Bloody Mary and dry, dry martinis.

Although it was Sally Quinn and the *Washington Post* who transformed the paunchy, bachelor into the most eligible male of the dullest administration socially speaking in history, it was Barbara Howar who snared him as her own, prize-winning, special bunny, escort and man-about town.

Everyone agreed that in taking up with Henry she performed a valiant service. Anything to relieve the deadly monotony of a town in which Barbara maintained "anyone out on the streets with a funny hat blowing a horn" could generate excitement. Miss Howar wasn't exactly magnanimous in her motives. She had just been divorced from a Lebanese husband who had possessed her fiercely. She was revelling in the flush of freedom, the excitement of independence when there was Henry standing right on her living room carpet, a canape in one hand, a cocktail in the other. Whatever her emotional yearnings to remain free and unencumbered, Barbara knew better than to let an eligible bachelor escape, especially an articulate, witty one capable of saying, what was it? Oh, yes, "just assume I'm a secret swinger."

In her own enormously entertaining book *Laughing All the Way* Barbara wrote: "From the time Richard Nixon took office, Henry Kissinger was the solitary accessible power figure in Washington. It was as though the hierarchy of Republicanism needed a key figure on which to focus during the reign of Richard Nixon. Had it been necessary to invent Henry, they could not have done a better job. Between the power of the President and the power of the press, Kissinger became an overnight legend. They got a lot of help from Henry."

Maintaining she made no apologies for Henry, Miss Howar went on. "Though I disagreed with, even loathed his politics, I had a decidedly friendly attitude toward him. As the man overrode his Dr. Strangelove stereotype, I stopped making fumbling apologies to liberals for consorting with the enemy."

Gloria Steinem enjoyed him too and she once flipped, "If this were the Kennedy administration nobody would pay attention to him. Barbara Walters said, "You keep hearing about the great charm he has with single glamorous ladies. But he's equally charming with married women and with men. And you always have the feeling that he's told you ten percent more than he has to."

In the weeks following his "coming out," Henry could be seen at more and more cocktail parties. When he arrived at the Situation Room the Katzenjammer Kids, neither of whom drank or smoked, often smelled whiskey on his breath and there were telltale signs of fatigue in Henry's bloodshot eyes—so red that they pierced the thick lens of his glasses.

Personally they may have been offended, but the Kissinger act had turned into a good one. It was playing well in Washington and it hadn't been banned in Peoria. As a matter of fact the yokels were lapping up accounts of Kissinger's antics and the general feeling was that the portly professor was doing his country as much good on his social peregrinations as in diplomatic situations. In any event the slot of sex symbol was open in the Nixon administration and there for Henry's taking. He grabbed it.

Henry obviously enjoyed the parties and turned out to be a Washington innovator. For a man in his position he didn't appear to care much where he was invited or by whom. As long as it promised to be interesting. He didn't stand on protocol and had long ago gotten over his insistence on being called Doctor. "Henry" was good enough for him —as long as someone called his name and she was young and pretty, a little on the tallish side, with good legs and some mode of conversation that would last through a soiree.

He was properly Bavarian in his post-party niceties, always sending flowers to the hostess next day. He never kept hostesses worried about accepting, answering calls promptly and with Teutonic thoroughness. He arrived late for briefings— on time or nearly on time for fun and games. He brought the lovely ladies who came to know him during this period lovely presents from abroad— caviar from Russia, silks from China, other goodies. He was an indefatigable post card sender— although his messages were harder to decipher than the codes the diplomat worked in.

The discovery of Henry Kissinger by Washington turned out to be a welcome breath of fresh air —a joy for everyone—especially the star himself. Henry Kissinger could not have felt that now he really "had it made." That was true of many situations he'd been thrust into before—by the combination of fate and his own acumen. But this time charisma was involved—*Baverische suesslichkeit*, if you will—and that was vastly different.

Henry could feel that he really, *really* had it made. He was the second most powerful man in the world and able to enjoy his jollies with the relish of a millionaire playboy. He probably pitied Haldeman and Ehrlichman—not because they would have enjoyed his life style—but because they would never have known how to go about it.

Washington girls were scornful of the Nixon men. Said one, "They were serious, hardworking humorless men. It is doubtful that they ever uttered an original line or thought an original thought. They dressed like college grads trying to make good on Madison Avenue—twenty years ago. There wasn't a sideburn in the bunch." "My God!" a newspaper woman hissed when she first saw Bob Haldeman, "He must be the only man in America who still wears a crew cut."

Being the very antithesis of his colleagues on the *Trio of Huns* was just another turn of the wheel for Henry. He was born lucky and, as the Chinese say, "Throw a lucky man into the sea, and he will come out with a fish in his mouth."

On the other hand, Henry's boss was typical of the born loser. They never know if they've won, according to psychiatrists, because they don't feel deserving of victory. They must surround themselves with the accounterments of victory—in Nixon's case, a huge personal staff, retreats in Key Biscayne and San Clemente, a palace guard, airplanes and helicopters—not forgetting those *Mittel Europa* uniforms for the White House police. They must keep reminding themselves and others that they have won. ("Make no mistake about it; I am the President.")

"Nixon," said psychiatrist Melvin Mandel, "always wanted to get to the White House, but he never knew what he wanted to do when he got there. He could never relax and enjoy the fruits of his victory."

Gloria Steinem, Sally Quinn and Barbara Howar rescued Henry from the Nixon jaws just in time. When he got around to enjoying the fruits of his victory. Kissinger was the fellow who turned Adam's apple-eating caper into an international picnic.

PART THREE

D.C. and Hollywood: Sex In the Afternoon

Life definitely changed for Henry "Secret Swinger" Kissinger. "Now, when I bore people," he said, "they think it's their fault."

CHAPTER THREE

"Henry Kissinger struck a blow for the personal liberty of politicians," one admirer of the man if not the political image exclaimed. "He's the best thing that happened to the country since the Kennedys showed people that the White House was a place to live in and be enjoyed. Every time a Kennedy tossed someone into the pool they were doing it vicariously for a lot of Americans who were weary of idols with secret clay feet. We've been hypocrites long enough and if a pudgy, bespectacled man can lead us out of the mire of deceit I, for one, an eager to follow him."

"Americans get so bloody uptight about their politicians," an English newspaperman once remarked. "I remember an American correspondent who was in England doing a series on our Parliamentary system and he was surprised to hear all over London that the Prime Minister was a transvestite. What's more he owned a perfectly brilliant woman's wardrobe and showed it to friends who knew his fetish on the slightest povocation.

"'Gawd!' gasped the American "What *Confidential* or the tabloids would explode over this! How come they don't do something about it over here? Hint at it, maybe.' I explained why not. The libel laws, for one thing, are fantastically strict in England. For another, did any one really care? In a little country like England lots of people knew about the fellow. What interested them was that he turned out to be a damned capable Prime Minister—in skirts or out of them."

About the nearest the United States ever came to official endorsement of sexual ambivalence occurred during the Roosevelt administration when an aide repeated what F.D.R. had heard thousands of times, that one of his Cabinet was a busy and not too circumspect homosexual. F.D.R. said, "Yes, I know and I've talked to him about it. I warned him to be sure he didn't practice it on government time."

Private morality does not enjoy the same scrutiny universally that makes it so near and dear to the American heart. It is surprising how little people outside the puritanical United States really care about what their neighbors do in bed. As for lawmakers abroad, most of them feel they have enough on their hands trying to solve parking problems and collect taxes without debating penalties for so-called morals offenses.

Italian officials, for example, will never understand the furor over the repeal of the country's ban on divorce. It was written into law only to satisfy an important and wealthy constituency, the Catholic Church. Since everyone ignored it, what difference did a statute make that kept the Church happy?

To the male chauvinists of Parliament, enjoying the benefits of an endless supply of mistresses who could not hope to badger them into divorcing their ever lovin' little women, the lifting of the divorce ban was a cruel blow, politically and personally. It merely renewed their convictions about the futility of legislating morality.

When Charles DeGaulle strode the world scene, the giant-sized President of France, there was no insult his enemies could hurl at him more devastating than "Puritan." DeGaulle, who neither smoked or drank, was a daily Communicant at Mass, lived with the same wife for half a century and never even took a mistress. As if his personal life were not embarrassing enough, he preached the same restraint to the French people. Hence the epithet, "Puritan," to summon French disgust, their almost forgotten hatred of the English with their warm beer and English *malaise* (which can be interpreted as anything from homosexuality to syphilis.)

The French and Italians have never forgiven Americans who, in the flush of the full-scale power they possessed in Europe after World War II, demanded that the legal houses of prostitution be closed down in those countries. The intent was to protect G.I.'s stationed abroad from their contaminating moral influence. The whores took to the street and the vile era of hustling began—with all its evils, mugging, V.D., even murder. On her death bed, the French woman politician-social worker, who clamored for the closing of red light districts throughout the country, got around to admitting she had made a grave mistake. No support for her confession was heard from the hard line American generals who supported her.

Historically, politicians have been a bawdy lot and their human frailties are taken for granted in most places. The average Britisher is still dismayed over the Profumo affair, totally incapable of understanding what was so evil about a Minister who circulated among call girls and attended a couple of sex orgies.

"Bloomin' lucky fellow" is the way most ordinary working men described their reaction. "Since he didn't give away any defense secrets, what was all the fuss about? They could have found that out in a couple of days and avoided all the nasty scandal. And what did John Profumo do anyway? Nothing that everyone else in the Government has been getting away with for years.

They never gave Nelson Rockefeller's mini-political "sex scandal" a chance to "play in Peoria" because that is the way Republicans do things, Rockefeller was shunted aside in the 1964 presidential campaign because the conservative wing was in the ascendancy and the powerful Republicans who represented it wanted to try on their boots with Barry Goldwater. They had little to lose against an incumbent like Lyndon Johnson, especially in view of their favorite son's controversial viewpoints. They were more afraid of a Rockefeller victory than a Goldwater defeat.

No solid basis existed for the convenient rumor that Rocky couldn't win because he had divorced a woman he'd been married to for many years and relinquished the custody of their children in order to marry a gay divorcee. Rocky and Happy weren't exactly Jack Kennedy's age—a time of life when a simple divorce could explode into a more overwhelming scandal. Most Americans accepted the Rockefeller situation for what it was—a marriage that reached a regrettable point of no return and stayed intact longer than it should have because of Rocky's prominence. As the Rockefellers avoided notoriety so did State Governors and Rockefeller happened to be an important one.

But the divorce had been discreetly handled, along with the new marriage. The press was uncommonly generous and so were New York voters. They didn't get excited about the purely personal affairs of the Rockefellers, and what would make them different from our now famous Peoria cousins? The polls showing Rocky a sure loser *solely* because of his divorce and remarriage weren't exactly convincing.

"Saint John the Righteous" Ehrlichman told the country and Senator Ervin's Committee investigating Watergate that right where he was sitting, in the sacred halls of Congress, there were often legislators who were so drunk they couldn't rise to their feet to answer a roll call. The Ervin Committee knew all about that—what they wanted to know was how deeply "John the Righteous" and the White House were implicated in the Watergate break-in. "At that point in time," Ehrlichman couldn't remember.

Ehrlichman's remarks were valid; the timing, inappropriate. He was neither spreading news or attacking the hypocrisy affecting the national capital. Washington is the drinkingest seat of government in the world. Everyone knows it and the District government has helped it along—like restricting drinking hours of public places and telling the drinker where to sit, what he should tuck in his stomach when he drinks and guiding him to moderation by any number of "do's" and "don'ts." To avoid confusion the Washingtonian wisely buys a bottle and takes it home and gets drunker.

D.C. is the land of sex in the afternoon. The town is filled with young women, unattached and available, who flock there from all parts of the country. When they start shopping around for government jobs they discover the rules in Washington vary little from those on Madison Avenue, show business or any other area where the emoluments of a career are measured both in terms of money and prestige.

Civil service takes care of the money; sex in the afternoon can mean promotion, marriage, a mistress situation—whatever the young lady desires. Women's Lib will one day eliminate the casting couch—and who is there to say that the emancipated ladies will welcome it? Not all. The girl with the imagination and determination to see out her "thing" is hardly the kind one considers a hayseed. One can assume that she knew the score beforehand and decided whether for her "the price was right."

Everything about Washington's sexual mores was geared for a challenge and the decision of Henry Kissinger to strike a blow for emancipation from his scholar's robes and high-minded devotion to an asexual White House. He'd been around

Washington long enough to realize that an unattached man enjoyed the automatic status of an Adonis.

His position spoke for itself. As an intellectual he rated attention for he represented a rare species during Republican administrations. Nora Ephrom wrote, "Henry Kissinger is genuinely charming, a nice man, self-depreciating, extremely thoughtful and kind. His wit may not be impressive by New York standards; indeed, it is probably best characterized as Teutonic. But for Washington, for a Republican official in Washington, no less, it seems astonishing.

"There are times when administration critics claim that Henry Kissinger's swinging image was a calculated plot designed to bring the Nixon group image some measure of life, humor, humanity even. From time to time a particularly virulent sniper suggested that Kissinger's dating of beautiful women—as, for example, during his trips to Paris—was simply a smoke screen to divert his attempts to negotiate with the Viet Cong. The critics were forced to lean on such improbable theories; how else to explain the improbable success of a 49-year-old German immigrant with large ears a commanding nose, frumpy clothes, wrinkled forehead, double chin and blooming paunch?

"As it turns out, however, there are other, simpler explanations. The first, and easiest, has to do with the media's stampede to cover anyone who might remotely be a human interest story. A second reason concerns the nature of life of any unattached man in Washington, D.C."

The press did wonders with Henry Kissinger and, as Barbara Howar pointed out, he enjoyed it. There was never anything shy about Henry when it came to publicity. This may seem at variance with his devotion to secrecy in diplomacy. But the Bavarian, like the Irish, is a braggart and while a man in Kissinger's sensitive position would never end up in a bar room brawl, drunkenly announcing how he negotiated with Ho Chi Minh, there were other ways to make the Kissinger personality known. And they went beyond *Time Magazine* covers which came to him automatically. Associating with beautiful women in the items of the gossip columns was one device to answer Henry's longing for approval as a man, a human being.

There was nothing tentative about Henry's dive into the sea of beautiful, fascinating, attractive women. He played the role of sexual *nouveau riche* to the hilt. Today, Washington, tomorrow the world became his slogan. When Washington hostesses got wind of his availability they were enchanted. Entertaining the Nixon people had become such a bore. Kissinger enchanted them right back. Even Democratic ladies who so despised the war he was championing.

Kissinger showed himself an astute diplomat on the canape circuit as in negotiating sessions. When he was called a "war-monger" by someone with a martini extra, Henry neither cried or left in a huff. Patiently he sat down and tried to explain his position all over again. He was the kind of rare Washington man-about-town you called "Henry" the first time you met him.

Life was definitely changing for Henry. "Now

when I bore people," Kissinger said, "they think it's *their* fault.

For a time the columnists had it that Henry was seriously taken with Gloria Stienem, and that could have been the intellectual match of the century. Tabloid readers—and editors—would have looked forward to the time of their lives. With politicians erasing movie stars from front pages as celebrities to gossip-hungry readers even the glorious Taylor-Burton headlines would have been overshadowed.

Unfortunately, Gloria would have nothing to do with it. That wouldn't have been playing fair with her followers, and she was right. Ms. Steinem made it a point to publicly deny a romance with Henry and enlarged her remarks to say: "These women (the Hollywood ladies) are not now, and never have been, old girl friends of Henry Kissinger."

Barbara Howar, the gal who started the whole Kissinger metamorphosis in the first place saw to it that Henry got around a lot and, in turn, Henry rewarded her with glimpses of the Government at work that she might not have seen otherwise. Barbara was no novice, of course, but the opportunity afforded her chances to see the difference in style between Johnson, Kennedy and Nixon.

Barbara has something curiously nice to say about Nixon in recalling Kissinger. "No one becomes a legend without penalties," she wrote. "Henry's has been to have his actions scrutinized day and night, by a tut-tutting public that appears to enjoy the sexual shenanigans of famous men a good deal more than it enjoys their accomplishments. I have to credit Nixon, unlike Kennedy and Johnson, who sought to control the private lives of their people. He hired Henry and turned him loose. I think he understood that when Henry shouted to bring in the dancing girls, Henry's only interest was in dancing."

Barbara admitted that eventually, she felt, Henry's playboy image began to wear a bit thin in the Oval Office. But, then, so did the oft-noted line in the newspapers, *Kissinger's foreign policy*. Nixon referred to Kissinger's nocturnal wanderings as appearances in "the liberal Georgetown cesspool." But at a time when his own morality was under heavy, unremitting fire, Nixon could only grin and bear the gossip and speculation about Henry's swinging, private life.

Warren Beatty is a handsome young man, a movie actor and producer, the brother of Shirley MacLaine and like Shirley, a political activist in the Democratic column. He campaigned for McGovern in the last presidential election and the shrieking fans who heard his speeches confessed later that they would have preferred the candidate himself—even "if he did sound like Liberace."

Whatever, Warren is a sincere sort of fellow as far as is known; like Henry Kissinger, a swinger with a reputation for loving his ladies and leaving them. Which may be one of the reasons that he admires Henry.

Talking to newsmen Beatty said, "Politicians are bigger stars than movie celebrities. Nobody gives a damn about actors any more. Public adora-

tion and hero worship has switched from film celebrities to political figures."

"Look at today's headlines and you have to realize that the term 'star' more befits today's politician than today's movie actor. Politicians, the men
with literally the power over life and death are the
new 'stars'. They're the new superhuman idols
that people now look to as glamorous. And they
are truly godlike and superhuman in their respon-
sibilities and world influence. They're our modern, bigger-than-life gods."

"Henry Kissinger is probably the world's most
popular 'star'. He has as much publicity or more
than any movie actor around. He travels a lot and
he enters into negotiations that affect people the
world over. How can the mythical heroism of a
film star compare to the international stature of
the politician? Even actors have become fans of
politicians. It gives them a thrill to rub shoulders
with some political giants like McGovern or Henry
Kissinger."

When Henry got around to it, he rubbed more
than shoulders with the movie stars for he was,
after all, Washington's *oomph* boy, the Jackie Onassis of the Nixon administration. But first he had
to attend to his knitting at the White House—and
that involved lots and lots of dropped stitches.

If Henry was the charmer of Washington's
cocktail and canape set, he was someone else in
the basement office he first occupied at the White
House. As he moved to ever better accommo-
dations in the next five years it reflected the increasing influence he obtained over President
Nixon.

To achieve his dominant position in the Administration, Kissinger moved sideways, backwards, to the left, to the right. There were times when he wiggled in so many directions that he seemed to be a dancing doll. And, of course, at the same time he was dodging enemies. Of itself Kissinger's opportunism was not evil. But staffers resented virtually everything about their boss, his arrogance, temper, impatience with human error, the shrill conviction of his own correctness. They could stomach all this. They were, after all, skilled Washington public servants. But they bitterly resented Kissinger's apple-polishing of the boss and they literally blanched at his fawning over the Katzenjammer Kids, Haldeman and Ehrlichman. This was tough on most of the top specialists Henry recruited for his National Security Council.

"He hired me in the back seat of a car going over to the Pentagon," said Roger Morris, an Africa expert from the Johnson Administration.

"He was cool. He said, 'I didn't support this guy either. I supported Rockefeller. But we're working for an institution here, the Presidency. We have to give the man a chance. He's going to make some major changes in foreign policy.'

"I guess I believed him", Morris said. "I wanted to believe him. Nixon at that point had said some promising things. In his first pep talk to the National Security Council he said, 'I know this place is impossible. Henry and I will end the war. I want you guys to run the rest of the world.' "

Let's step out of this narrative for a few paragraphs and slip back to that part of Roger Morris' account of his recruitment by Henry Kissinger, the part where a presidential aide refers to the President as "guy." "I didn't support this *guy* either." Morris obviously used it deliberately because he had remembered it and because few American displomats refer to the President as "guy."

If ever Kissinger committed a Bavarianism, this was it. It tells a great deal about the man, having to do with Bavarian attitudes and almost fanatic devotion to the colloquial in language, the suggestion of intimacy in their relations to those in authority and their own need to suggest superiority by speaking in terms of the "regular guy," the man on the street. Complicated? Yes, but so is the Bavarian.

Bavarians speak a rich, earthy, colorful dialect of which they are inordinately proud. In many respects it is altogether different from *hoch Deutsch*. It is a *Volksprache*—a people's language. And that is what they look for in a foreign language—the common denominator of language, the slang, the colloquial. Teach a Bavarian between "you and me" and let him hear "between you and I" in the neighborhood bar, and he will switch to the latter.

The North German, at least until World War II, saw a sharp distinction between what he called American and English-English. Being more exposed to "English-English" he chose to be accurate and as nearly perfect as possible. English-speaking Germans of the port *Hansastadt* of Hamburg, for example, have enjoyed centuries-old commerce with England and, despite the interruption of the Great Wars, their ties remained close. Hamburgers speak their own language with the precise, clipped diction of the English.

Today's Bavarian has heard more American than "English-English" and he loves it and, like Kissinger, sprinkles his use of the language with words like "guy"—not that they're slang but because they represent to him the American ideal, a casual, informal world where peasants mingle freely with Barons—as they do in Bavaria. That peasant meets Baron only when out walking their dogs doesn't occur to him.

In using common langue Kissinger seeks to escape the onus of appearing pendantic. He professes to prefer "Henry" to "Doctor" in society—but he seems to be saying that when it comes to the professional image, "Let's not forget the qualifying titles." Keeping up with the Kissinger foibles is no easy task. As they say in Germany, "The Berliner eats his wurst before the Bavarian has begun. That's to give the Berliner time to figure him out."

There were originally about a hundred specialists on Kissinger's staff in the Nixon Administration, and to a man they were liberals compared either to their immediate boss or to Nixon. Many were Democrats with fine records of service under Kennedy and Johnson. Within eighteen months most liberals were gone, yelling "foul." They claimed, with what proved to be ample justification, that they had been wiretapped. Kissinger had become fanatical about press leaks.

Morale in the basement workshop never

dropped because it had never been high to begin with. "Kissinger was one lousy administrator. He didn't know how to handle people" said one cranky specialist who quit within a few months.

"Henry recognizes quality and he recognized mediocrity and inferiority. He really would like to get the best people but he's got to get them on his own ground rules or he doesn't want them at all. His ground rules are that they are anonymous and that they work only for him and talk only to him and they don't goddam well participate in any process except in terms that have been laid down. As a result, he doesn't always get good men."

If Kissinger harassed his aides, the Special Assistant to the President, suffered, in turn, the harassment of the Katzenjammer Kids. Having seen them on television any Jewish mother would have asked herself what was a nice Jewish boy doing around them? If you can't tell a book by its cover, why do publishers go to so much trouble creating provocative covers? Ehrlichman and Haldeman not only looked like Gestapo agents they sounded like them.

Kissinger had felt their cold breath on his neck for years and he was one of the first Nixon appointees they fingered for "hanging in the breeze." It was never spelled out for Henry, but the White House policy in respect to Henry was that would never go "public" in the first Administration— that he would stay behind the scenes as the mastermind, thus veiling, if not concealing, his German-Jewish background.

A lot of White House staffers admired Kissinger. They respected his guts and, when they saw what he was doing, admired his persistence. Some among them wondered why he didn't quit. He could do without the job. He didn't need to endure the forced fellowship imposed by his association with Haldeman and Ehrlichman.

Then, there were the others, men of vision who believed Kissinger was formulating the best foreign policy available at the time and under the circumstances. He was shaping it, biding his time and doing his job. He had control of Nixon—and that was the equivalent of holding his finger over the buttons on the little black box.

"His strength was the media," said C. Fred Bergstein, a top economist who quit in 1971 because Kissinger ignored economic issues. "He handled the media well." "I wandered into his office one day and took a look at his schedule," said a newspaperman, "And there it was—an entire day of back-to-back talks with top Washington newmen who depended on Kissinger for the most solid information coming out of the Viet Nam war area."

But it was U.S. foreign policy itself, the invasion of Cambodia in 1970, the support of Pakistan's bloody assault on Bangladesh in 1971, the mining of Haiphong and the bombing of Hanoi in 1972, that Kissinger's former aides believe ultimately saved him from Ehrlichman and Haldeman. Kissinger approved the hardline policy in public, if not always privately.

On the afternoon of the Cambodia invasion, Kissinger told staffers, "Our leader has flipped his lid. But you're all expected to rally 'round. If you can't, get out. We can't have any carping in the back room."

Twelve Harvard professors came to protest Cambodia, but Kissinger refused to talk to them on the record. "He was trapped," said an aide, "he couldn't tell them what he was saying socially all over Washington, that Nixon was mad, that he had to humor an irrational man."

That was bold talk from a man beholden to a patron who happened to be the most powerful man in the world, and a number of reasons were advanced for his seeming recklessness. Of all the explanations—and they ranged far and wide—that he was shoring up his own position for the inevitable impeachment, that he was a tool of the left, protecting the left from the right—the simplest was put forward by actress Marsha Matrinko who said, "He manipulates people beautifully. You know it's happening but you like it. If you can stay with him witwise, you can have a ball."

Marsha once carried a title, and this may have titillated Bavarian-born Henry Kissinger. The tall honey blonde who dated Kissinger in Washington regularly and when he wasn't busy, in Paris, New York, Acapulco or Hollywood, used to be "Miss Love Bunny."

The Nixon people just loved San Clemente— the rolling sea, the quiet beach, the Secret Service that kept the common herd from polluting the Pacific waters, the hotel in town where they drank their cokes and swallowed vitamins and the presence of the Chief himself. It was a great way to spend those Nixon working vacations.

But that was not the way Henry saw it. Not for him—the steady sweep of the waves, the stars shining down on white sand. He preferred looking up to the stars in a different ambiance—the garish, neon bistros of Wilshire Boulevard, the Sunset Strip and other celebrated Hollywood locations. Horace Greeley knew what he was talking about when he said, "Go west, young man, go west." But since he didn't say where in the west, Henry was pleased to settle for Bel Air, Hollywood and Beverly Hills.

Henry Kissinger's jowls must have shaken with glee, his lips moistening with anticipation, as he looked forward to his first assault on Hollywood. Henry had the advantages of his reputation as a formidable Don Juan and status as one of the world's most important men. It's hard for anyone to top that—even a million-dollar-a-year movie star like Robert Redford.

As a student of history Henry must have recognized the significance of following in the footsteps of so many distinguished statesmen who enjoyed the heady thrill of placing their shoes under the beds of Hollywood beauties whose names belong to American folklore—courtesans equal in grace, charm and secret accomplishments to Napoleon's Josephine, Lola Montez and Nell Gwynn.

Henry's homework revealed the strong bonds that existed between Hollywood and Washington and, for that matter, Show Business at large—bonds forged in the White House itself and dipping down to the lowest jobholder in the bureaucracy. Politics and the performing arts have much in common, both being the products of artifice and make-believe. As well as living on the generosity and appreciation of the public.

Show Business long recognized the wisdom of buttering up politicians and showing appreciation for favors rendered by extending the courtesy of the profession—say, a bit of hanky-panky with a starlet, on the house. It worked like a charm in settling small problems, like building law violations, or killing the rap sheet of a big star nabbed for drunk driving. Supplying contributions and star power to big campaigns succeeded for years in bottling up the anti-trust laws, enabling the early film tycoons to create a monopoly that made them millionaires many times over.

The gossip circuit for years has been titillated by the amorous antics of Washington and Show Biz—going back in this century to the Administration of Woodrow Wilson, who made no secret of his admiration for vaudeville and its lovely young girls who travelled from city to city singing and dancing their way into the hearts of lovely middle-aged men they called "Johns," "Sugar Daddies" and "Stage Door Johnnys." Until President Wilson married for the second time, the housekeeping staff considered constructing a revolving door to handle the traffic between the local vaudeville houses and the White House—so many were the pretty singing and dancing ladies who came to call.

Al Jolson sang songs like "Uncle Sam Needs Warren Harding" which wasn't true at all. The country could have done quite well without him, and we can imagine that Al really wasn't all that knowledgeable about President Harding. What with playing around with Nan Britten in the White House linen closet he couldn't have noticed that he was giving the country away to his crooked Cabinet members. Calvin Coolidge helped Will Rogers gain national prominence with his impersonation of "Silent Cal", but it remained for Herbert Hoover, of all people, to really make a marriage of convenience with Hollywood.

His great and good friend was movie tycoon Louis B. Mayer who, unlike Hoover, was a swinger. Mayer pouted, for instance, when Jeanette MacDonald refused to sit on his lap when they talked over her new contract. "All the other girls do," he said petulantly.

Miss MacDonald stood firm, but she was the exception. The gals around Metro-Goldwyn-Mayer, the studio Mayer lifted to the pinnacle of achievement during his despotic reign as its "guiding genius" did pretty much what L.B. wanted them to —and that included going to the capital when they were told, supporting Hoover against Roosevelt in 1932, as well as a lot of other things.

That Roosevelt knocked Hoover out of the White House by a landslide was not the kind of defeat to dismay Louis B. for very long. If he was known as Mr. Republican out in Culver City, there was Jack Warner over in Burbank who could pass for a Democrat any day of the week. And Mayer promptly installed a few token Democrats in top echelon positions at the studio. So whoever ran things in Washington—or Sacramento—or New York (which housed the executive and sales offices)—made very little difference to the movie companies. There was enough good cheer, ex pense money, contributions and flesh to go around. Starlets cost $75 a week on seven year contracts whose options were controlled solely by the studios. They were joyously passed from bed to bed and were certainly available to "honored guests."

Hollywood was truly a beautiful place when F.D.R. took office in the thirties—a gorgeous, smogless playground whose nocturnal diversions were as famous as its natural resources, the sea, the mountains, the desert and the lakes. And to it flocked the beautiful people—young girls from everywhere who, if they didn't make it to a stock contract, could be found hoisting trays at drive-ins, dazzling the customers with their luscious smiles and mini-skirt costumes.

At night, the name *Hollywoodland* lighted up the skies on the Hollywood Hills and there were fun and games to be had at the Cocoanut Grove, the Biltmore Bowl, the Trocadero on the fledgling Sunset Strip and soon there would come Ciro's, the Clover Club, and fine restaurants that the Hollywood columnists doted on describing as "eateries"—Romanoff's, Dave Chasen's, LaRue and many others.

Because Roosevelt couldn't come to Hollywood, Hollywood went to Roosevelt in the White House. The stars were there for his birthdays, the March of Dime campaigns, for the inaugurations, the special events, the war rallies, the bond drives—whatever F.D.R. wanted, F.D.R. got. And that included beautiful girls. He had a huge reservoir of charm to pass around, and he liked most of all to share it with pert, young things.

And the Roosevelt people flocked to Hollywood. Elliott even became a film producer and married Faye Emerson, and Mrs. Roosevelt paid frequent visits to the film colony, ostensibly to visit him and her daughter, Anna, who lived in nearby Seattle. She frankly enjoyed the change from stuffy Washington, the informality, the give-and-take of the Baghdad-by-the-sea. She stood in a Hollywood theatre at a premiere one night and heard the fans gasp, "Why, she's beautiful." A Hollywood make-up man and a hairdresser, sent to Mrs. R. by one of the studios, had indeed done a magical job. She was beautiful—and her radiant personality helped the illusion along.

The son of Roosevelt aide Harry Hopkins, David, maried one of the Preisser dancing sisters. And when the war clouds hovered over Europe and drifted toward the Pacific, there came the generals and other government brass. They all wanted to visit the studios and Louis B. Mayer, Jack Warner, the Schenk Brothers, Darryl Zanuck even cranky Harry Cohn, the Last Tycoon of Columbia, greeted them warmly.

The starlets enjoyed the pick of anything in wardrobe for their gala nights out, and there were all sorts of comings and goings at the various posh hotels around town and in the motels that sprouted up in that song-celebrated area, the San Fernando Valley.

World War II brought the Madams to Hollywood and a chain of communication was established between the movie capital and Las Vegas with "Bugsy" Siegel and any number of minor and major hoods in charge. No one was surprised because the hoods and the Madams were vital to the Hollywood way of doing things. The studios needed those bare necessities of life, then in short supply—steaks, gas coupons, champagne, fine whisky, late model cars, silk stockings, white shirts; well, just about everything. Even money. There were wartime limits on earned income, so a flourishing black market in U.S. dollars cropped up. Dozens of independent movies of the era were financed totally by cash, and stars nearly dropped their choppers when, at week's end, some hood stopped by with envelopes stuffed with hundred dollar bills instead of the paychecks usually delivered to their agents.

The price of starlets went up to a hundred and fifty a week—with the little pluses they received for special favors. Fur coats, bright stones, war bonds—things that made a girl happier in her job.

If the walls of those Beverly Hills-Bel Air mansions and the San Fernando Motels could talk! What wondrous tales they would spin of Four Star Generals, Navy braid, Special Assistants, Congressional Liaisons, Cabinet Members on top secret missions, Congressmen "investigating" and small fry who got attention just because they looked good. This was an era when Hollywood knew the wisdom of the old Mark Hellingerism, "Be nice to the people on the way up, you never know when you're going to meet them on the way down."

It took Harry Truman a while to connect with Hollywood but when he did it was the beginning of an enduring love affair.

Hollywood was at its glittering best when Margaret Truman came to Hollywood Bowl and sang.

Like they said—more stars than there are in heaven—showed up, and Margaret didn't conquer. But that didn't really matter—she was the President's daughter and a charming one who one day would get over her private vanity about her voice and settle into the self-possessed, intelligent matron she is today. Hollywood made no mistake in putting its best foot forward in a warmly honest welcome.

As Louella Parsons would have said it, the Kennedys relieved the "deadly dullness" of the Eisenhower years and Hollywood eagerly embraced the young, handsome new President and his entourage, looking forward to a rerun of the Golden Days. There was little of Jackie but more of Jack and Bobby who splashed in the surf at Santa Monica and gave Peter Lawford a social standing he'd been on the edge of but never managed before, despite marriage to a Kennedy.

It was a different, fragmented Hollywood than the Golden Era of Louis B. Mayer. There weren't even any stock girls under contract. The movie studios had been gone and there were dozens of little companies. You couldn't tell one star from the other. They all looked alike. Naturally, the Kennedys preferred the traditional glamor girls—like Marilyn Monroe.

She was to die under circumstances that would billow into one of the great mysteries of the century—produced by the telephone calls Marilyn made on the night she succumbed to an overdose. What were the numbers she dialed? Who were the people she telephoned? Was one of them a Kennedy? Why were the records of her phone calls destroyed by the telephone company?

Who was being protected? The President of the United States or his brother, Bobby?

None of the principals in the mystery are alive today to answer those questions, and the mystery lingers on—like one of the movies Hollywood was famous for.

Because of their opposition to the war in Viet Nam the beautiful people of Hollywood sat out the Johnson Administration—leaving the hawks to run the place: John Wayne, Ward Bond, Hedda Hopper, until she died, and the rich directors and producers who checked under the bed every night for Communist spies.

Carol Channing, about as asexual as they come, offered a note of Show Bix to fellow Texan L.B.J., by paraphrasing her "Hello, Dolly" to "Hello, Lyndon" and campaigning for him in the 1964 election campaign. Carol was a champion, holding on to White House ties for her profession. Carol proved a thoroughbred by making the Nixon "enemies list." It was a moment of triumph, and Carol savored it on talk show after talk show as she scampered around the country, plugging her night club engagements.

Richard Nixon may have gained Frank Sinatra and Sammy Davis, Jr. in the 1972 presidential sweepstakes but Nixon had to realize that it was "no dice" as far as the new beautiful people were concerned, Shirley MacLaine, Paul Newman, Joanne Woodward and virtually all the kids like Jane and Peter Fonda. It should have been a blow to California-born Richard Nixon except that he had come to view Hollywood, like Georgetown, as a "moral cesspool." What Governor Ronald Reagan had ever seen in the place he couldn't understand which may have proved that Nixon really stuck close to the football games and reruns of "Patton" for entertainment. If he had seen Regan's B. movies he might have understood the extraordinary rewards available in Hollywood to what was definitely a non-talent.

Friendship with Frank Sinatra used to assure the visitor to Hollywood many things—a ride in his helicopter, a trip to Palm Springs, an evening with the Rat Pack or what was left of it, but not any more. Not since Sammy Davis embraced Richard Nixon. That meant losing Rosalind Russell, Peter Lawford, Lauren Bacall—among the old-timers and a slew of new names that hadn't been especially impressed with *Ole Blue Eyes* in the first place. Not even his records.

So when Henry Kissinger first arrived in Hollywood he chose to play it cool—avoiding the Nixonites and taking up with non-controversial Anne and Kirk Douglas, two socially minded individuals, Democrats, but also realists. When not counting his money Kirk can be a mighty brainy fellow, sincerely interested in a number of things, from ecology to improving the subway in his native New York. He worries about Brownsville and the underprivileged countries with equally serious expressions—the same grim face, dimple and teeth, the jutting jaw that have made him a world-famous movie star. Being a producer has made him a millionaire as well. So Kirk talks a good cause—and with good reason.

Aware that he is wearing himself out as an actor, disinclined to grace Broadway again where he wasn't exactly hailed some years back in *One Flew Over the Cuckoo's Nest*. Kirk nurses ambitions to do something along diplomatic lines— maybe a portfolio as Roving Ambassador to Space. Failing that, he would settle for anything on earth, as long as it didn't effect his pocketbook.

What better way to fan those ambitions than by currying favor with that man called Kissinger, distinguished advisor to the President?

Kirk is not the kind of man to allow his private political opinion of the Nixon regime to interfere with his social activities. He has even maintained friendly relations with John Wayne—a feat in itself.

Kirk Douglas goes back to the Forties in Hollywood, an old-timer by today's standards, and no one ever figured on his becoming a social leader in the community. An actor, millionaire producer, an egoist who talks about himself in the third person, yes. A social leader, no.

It began in 1954 when he married his second wife, Anne Buydens,° a French woman, who scraped together a postwar living as a publicist, then a comparatively new profession in France. One of her accounts was the Cannes Festival, and she handled it with grace and distinction. Anne became Kirk's secretary when he made a picture in Paris in the Sixties, a disaster best forgotten called *Act of Love* in which he co-starred with Dany Robin. They were cast as star-crossed young lovers of the Occupation, Kirk, as a G.I.; Dany, as a young French girl. Both were too old for the parts and one wag suggested that the movie would have made a fine vehicle for Marjorie Main and Percy Kilbride.

But a marriage came out of the assignment and Anne assiduously guided Kirk into the cultural and social level she lived in. His own ambitions for acceptance matched hers, and they rank today at the very tiptop of Hollywood society. Both, however, recognized cleavage as an essential ingredient to the success of a Hollywood party, so when they gave an affair for Henry Kissinger on one of his first trips to movieland, they invited Jill St. John to supply it.

Jill, at the moment, was involved with, as they say in the Hollywood columns, "none other than Frank Sinatra" and it was on his arm that she arrived. at the Kirk Douglas soiree. *Quelle soiree!*

Henry took one look at the statuesque lady, and her cleavage and that was the end of his diplomatic reserve. "He went ape," said one observer. "He couldn't keep his eyes off her. He was like a kid standing at the window of a candy store with a penny in his pocket looking at the five dollar box of chocolates."

Which brings to mind what a friend once said of Henry, "He's the creep nobody would ever eat lunch with. He was the kind of kid other kids would steal a candy bar from out of pure meanness. He had a terrible childhood. He was a grind and inevitably thought of himself as a hopelessly asexual person. Give a fellow in that state of mind some power and he does indeed go ape. There's nothing else for him to do, no place to go.

And to show his power—and convince himself of something he needs, confidence—he makes a play for the prettiest thing in the room."

This happened to be Miss St. John. The technique worked, and within a comparatively short period of time they were seen all over town together, constant companions at lunch, dinner, night clubs. She became the first well-known actress Kissinger met.

Jill St. John explained why it all happened. "Men I like have two things in common. They are smart and they have power. They also must have strong personalities. Henry is really my best male friend. I can call him at three in the morning with my problems and talk to him for hours and hours and he won't mind."

The exact nature of Miss St. John's problems never came to light but one thing seemed fairly certain. They didn't involve money. Jill was born Jill Oppenheim in Los Angeles and was thirty-one when she met Kissinger. She had led a busy life, professionally, intellectually and emotionally.

Hollywood became aware of Jill on two counts; her beauty and mind. She had—and presumably still does—a high I.Q. which was reported in the Hollywood columns with the respect such an attribute deserves. Her first matrimonial venture was at age seventeen. She married and divorced two millionaires, Neil Rubin and Lance Reventlow, obtaining huge settlements from both. She evidenced her I.Q. by saying, "I much prefer settlements. Alimony is so untidy." Then she married Jack Jones, an affable young singer, riding a wave of popularity at the time. They became Jack and

Jill—but that was about all. They divorced almost at the altar.

Jill's marriage to Jack failed to win the approval of his father, singer Allen Jones, an easy-going, likable man normally disinclined to interject himself into his son's private affairs. Lance Reventlow's fascination with the lady known as Jill threw his mother, heiress Barbara Hutton, into a frenzy and she didn't rest easy until it was over and the settlement agreed to and paid for.

Jill's escorts have been a colorful lot of rich, famous men and provided ammunition for coverage in the columns that always notes the St. John personality—and appurtenances. Her collection of jewelry appears to have only one rival—Paulette Goddard's and Jill put it together a lot faster. She divides her time among several homes she reportedly owns outright. Her clothes are fabulous and she dotes on fast, custom-made cars. Jill has been called a character right out of Harold Robbins.

Whatever, she fascinated Henry Kissinger whose eyes bulged whenever he glimpsed Jill and her cleavage in low-cut gowns and doubtless he longed for television-telephone to make those nocturnal advice-seeking sessions more provocative.

At one time Jill's press agent reported they were going to Mexico together where Kissinger had some business of state. There were denials from his office but the press, suspecting a marriage, dogged them both to the point that the weary diplomat decided to carry on alone. There was always the telephone to tie him to Jill and her problems.

For a woman, who had been taking care of herself since she was a kid and a television performer,

Jill made two fatal mistakes in dealing with Henry. She was violently anti-Nixon, having gone on record with some nasty statements about the President. After taking note of his settling in San Clemente, she described Orange County as the most reactionary in the state. "It deserves Nixon." This, of itself, wasn't an error, at least not one Henry couldn't live with. He valued his Democratic friends more than his Republican colleagues. They broke the terrible monotony of the stuffy political ambiance in which he circulated. But she persisted in talking about the war—when Henry had other things on his mind.

That didn't set well at all. Henry was a busy man, and while it was tough separating himself from the problems of the lady and the undoubted fact that she certainly was a decorative thing to float around town with, he had other fish to fry. Fish that didn't talk quite as much and weren't nearly as opinionated as the gal with all that I.Q.

Jill's second mistake was introducing Henry to Joyce Haber, a friend and Hollywood columnist. Had she asked old-timer Kirk Douglas he would have warned her. But it was too late. Joyce dated Henry a couple of times, largely in her professional capacity.

At this point the parade of beauties started. Joyce promptly fixed Henry up with a number of other actresses—Sammantha Eggar, Joanna Barnes, Marlo Thomas, Candice Bergen. On his own he managed various encounters with Judy Brown, star of the Danish X-rated movie, *Threesome*. He also was involved with the Gabors—which didn't require special skills.

162

Not all of Henry Kissinger's friends/enemies were disquieted by his romantic jousting. "After all, after a day with Golda Meir, a man deserves someone like Jill St. John at night," commented one in a thoughtful moment.

Joyce Haber quickly explained to her readers the true Henry and Jill situation. The star hadn't exactly been given her walking papers when he moved into new territory. She was permitted to linger on—sort of a *voyeur* in the Kissinger capers.

Lada Edmond, for instance, is a tantalizing blonde in her late twenties who enjoys a fine reputation and considerable skill as a lady stunt girl. Her fees run into four figures for such stunts as driving cars into brick walls, falling down stairs, ducking bullets by way of skyscraper windows and falling off motorcycles. Her acting experience, at the time she met Henry, was limited to appearances in a couple of soft-core movies like *Revolt of the Female Chain Gang*. Lada remembered spending an evening with Jill and Henry.

"He was really coming on strong," she said, "I thought it was a little weird because there was Jill sitting right there. But he and Jill seemed to have a strange relationship. They seemed to get off on each other's sexual achievements."

Kissinger asked Lada for a date. She vetoed it at first, but Jill urged her to accept. Finally she agreed. Henry got extremely nervous, though, when Lada jokingly suggested that she pay for the night on the town since being seen with him would be good for her career. "I think someone in charge of the store had told him to cool it."

Back on the Potomac Richard Nixon was forced into an ambivalent attitude toward his special advisor. His administrative need for Henry was painfully obvious. Apart from the wire-tap thing he remained the only *Mr. Clean* in the White House. One by one Congress and the courts were hacking away at the Presidential staff, and replacements automatically labored under the tainted images of their predecessors.

Nixon, pushed ever closer to the ropes, was hardly in a position to belabor his most valued advisor, the man he was counting on to become Secretary of State, about his private affairs. Kissinger, no less than his enemies, had placed his boss in an uncomfortable position. He couldn't, by the very nature of his work, remain locked way away in the White House basement, contributing the most important papers of the Nixon Administration, and still preserve his anonymity. He'd grown less fearful of speaking in public and now met the people straight on by means of television.

Too, Henry had shored up a great deal of good will among the press. After a doubtful start and in view of all the secrecy he employed, Kissinger was eventually able to impress newsmen with the reasons behind all the cloak and dagger stuff. They chose to believe him.

Then, his private life gave some spice to their work. It was good to have someone around the Nixon staff unafraid to be himself, obviously enjoying his role of overstuffed Don Juan and pleased to be the clown. He'd come a long way since he admitted being a "secret swinger."

Kissinger also had accurately gauged the temperament of America. They had wearied of the antiseptic phoniness of the Nixonites. Middle-aged Republicans had seen enough long hair around to consider it nearly normal and the frequent TV appearances of Ziegler, Ehrlichman and Haldeman began to grate. Americans, Kissinger knew, can be very uptight about their neighbors' morality, but they prefer no one to notice. They want to be presumed as broadminded and as unbiased as the laws of the land say they're supposed to be.

So Kissinger began to show himself to the public-at-large in a more favorable light. Besides being the one "guy" in Washington who got things done he had become positively likable. And since he was European, that explained a lot of things.

Kissinger's offstage behavior amounted to giving Americans a welcome glimpse of the European political scene where foreign ministers are assumed to have mistresses even if they don't, and a delicate liaison with a beautiful lady is taken for granted, even admired.

People had begun to read about F.D.R. and Lucy Rutherford—and brought back memories of his years in office when the story circulated freely that the President had an old-time love tucked away in his cupboard. It wasn't *really* believed, because no one wanted to.

Then, there was the scandal that the Squire of Hyde Park had become so taken with one of the young girls close to the Dutch Royal Family that he had virtually promised her the Allies would invade through the Nazi-occupied Low Countries. Even the doubters among reporters had to fall back on the old highway to fact, "Where there's smoke there's fire."

About the only official cognizance of Kissinger's peccadillos came when it was suggested that he be just a little more circumspect in his choice of companions while on the Potomac cocktail circuit. It seems that there was nothing naive or unsophisticated about the reaction of the African underdeveloped countries to Henry's reputation as a Casanova. The manipulators of one African delegation decided they needed the ear of someone closer to the President than the officials they usually approached. Enter Monique, a tall, handsome, exotic African woman of almost incredible beauty and taste, a lady who sent out sex waves as she entered a room.

Monique found it easy to gravitate to Henry, and he certainly didn't reject what was obviously a play for him. Unaccustomed to that approach, Henry was naturally flattered. He responded to Monique with typical enthusiasm and, we can assume, with his usual vitality. It got to the point that Monique and Henry were beginning to be noticed. And a rival African Embassy decided it was time to step in as the spoiler. Word was discreetly sent to the State Department, accustomed to that sort of thing. They delighted in it. It had been years since a *femme fatale* near-scandal had come their way. It was a relief from the commonplace preoccupation of what they had been told to call the "third rate burglary at Watergate."

The State Department fiddled around and managed to lay their hands on Monique's passport and discovered that is was flawed. She was urged to pack up her beautiful gowns and jewel caskets and head back for Africa, unless she wanted to risk an incident. In her impeccable French, Monique smiled "*Oui, je comprend*" and nearly swayed the State Department junior officer in charge into calling the whole thing off. She disappeared abruptly from the social scene, and Henry, ever the discerning diplomat, pretended not to notice.

Employing a beautiful woman to beguile an international political figure was the kind of plot assumed to have gone out of style in the eighteenth century. The saga of sultry Monique and Henry, however, was taken for granted, par for the course in these unpredictable times. Another notch in Henry's belt, a touch of tabasco to the Kissinger mystique.

The press had created a number of nicknames for the flamboyant, secretive diplomat; each, in its fashion, revealing one of Kissinger's many faces—"Dr. Strangelove," "Superkraut," "Novel Warrior," "Reluctant Wiretapper" and "The Playboy of the Western Wing."

Kissinger had become a regular in the Gallup polls, continually rated high among the men that Americans admired most in the world. For a time, early in 1964 when his boss' popularity was at its nadir, Kissinger stood at the top of the Gallup sampling. Abroad Kissinger enjoyed the sort of celebrity status heretofore known only to movie stars. In some places he had become a cult hero, his round, expressive face drawing more instant recognition in many nations than the local ruler.

Government leaders, like so many shy fans, inveigled ways to be photographed with him—especially the Arab Sheiks who were frankly fascinated with the accounts of his romantic prowess and dates with beauties who were well known to them through TV, movies and photographs, Jill St. John and Marlo Thomas.

At a conference of Western Hemisphere foreign ministers held in Mexico City, Kissinger was so sought-after by his Latin counterparts that they even followed him into the men's room. The Mexico City newspaper dutifully headlined, *Kissinger Confers in W.C.*

Kissinger's exalted reputation as a wonder-worker would never have been forged had not Richard Nixon been hampered and crippled by Watergate. Nixon, of all presidents, feared competition in his Administration, and certainly the quality of his appointees reflected the man's own insecurity. He constantly protected his own position by mediocrity—and eventually it was the mediocrity of the people around Nixon which ruined him. Kissinger became the architect of U.S. policy by default. He was the right man in the right place at the right times, said London *Times* Foreign Editor Louis Heren. "Much of the world, East as well as West, hankers for a Superman. The role was thrust upon him, although presumably he did not have to be persuaded."

Kissinger's domination of the international scene evoked mixed reactions. "He is a trouble-maker out of the Nineteenth Century," snapped a ranking French Gaullist. Israel's Deputy Premier Rigil Allon (one of his former students) described

Kissinger's diplomatic skills more favorably, "He does his homework. He is a master of detail, a man with a quick mind and an acute sense of timing."

From Joe Sisco, an Assistant Secretary of State for Near Eastern and South Asian affairs, came this tribute: "Maybe it can't be done, but if anybody can do it, Kissinger can."

Attorney General John Mitchell called him an "egotistical maniac." Then there was the secretary who asked for his autograph saying, "He's *suess*, a courtier," using the German word for sweet with its sugary overtone. Minor government officials have been known to hang around the Kissinger presence, simply for the opportunity to shake his hand and say "hello."

Flushed with the success of his Paris negotiations with Hanoi's Le Duc Tho (whom he called "Ducky") Kissinger sat down and explained how he felt about his own mystique to Italian journalist Oriana Fallaci. Said Kissinger, "Americans admired the cowboy leading the caravan astride his horse, the cowboy entering the village alone, without even a pistol, because he doesn't go in for shooting."

Kissinger's "High Noon" act tripped him up near the end of the Vietnam peace talks in 1972 when he appeared on TV to announce "Peace is at hand" three months too early. "He was in such a high that he blew his cool," said Fred Bergsten who saw him that week. "He thought he had a deal, and Nixon overturned it because it was a Kissinger deal. And because Kissinger never mentioned Nixon at the press conference." But Melvin

Laird, who was then Nixon's Pentagon chief, contended that "Henry was pressed into overselling the peace deal to make it into a grand thing as we neared the election in 1972."

It was a major goof, but Kissinger survived it where a President would have been slaughtered in the public opinion polls. Consider how often in the years of his Administration Franklin Roosevelt was haunted by his "I hate war" speech. It is still listed by his enemies as one of Roosevelt's high crimes.

In his artless way Kissinger was right in comparing himself to the lone cowboy. He was the superstar of a pitiful group of people, trying to hold together a government riddled with corruption, deceit and vulgarity. The American people had to admire someone, so they chose Henry Kissinger.

The scene became familiar—four trips to eleven nations, for instance, when Henry swings around the globe on one of his tours.

It begins at eight o'clock in the morning when one by one the ambassadors of the countries Kissinger intends visiting, arrive to see him off. There are handshakes all around, and then the big blue and white Air Force One heads out over the Atlantic.

Kissinger's is a tight and very different ship from that presided over by Secretary of State William Rogers, who spent the long hours in the air playing bridge. Now and then Kissinger strolls back to the press section to talk to reporters, but not for attrition.

Arriving at its destination the door of the plane swings open and out pops a wavy-haired, pudgy man of less than average height with the unmistakable aura of a true celebrity, adjusting his glasses and his smile, the visitor speaks in a solemn baritone, the scholarly sentences laced, to the puzzlement of some, with the Germanic accents of his native Bavaria. The hopes, fears and future of his own country and the world appear to depend on what is about to transpire—who Kissinger will see, what will be said, how he will react, what new proposals will be offered.

They used to say in the great days of Hollywood that everyone had two businesses—his own and the movies. Kissinger, virtually single-handed, has changed all that. Today everyone has, besides his own operation, affairs of state to worry about. Even the change of Administrations, the dilemma of inflation and the furor over the Nixon pardon and Viet Nam amnesty proposal have not dimmed America's keen interest in foreign affairs. The oil mess has helped Kissinger stay in the spotlight. How long he will remain there poses something of a puzzlement, but that was furthest from Henry's mind in the grand and glorious days of his diplomatic legerdemain.

Kissinger's dizzy diplomatic successes failed to quench his appetite for either the jolly good time of the British or the popular divertisements of the Middle East in which he virtually took up permanent residence for so many weeks. He found time to relax in the belly dancing night clubs that flourish in Cairo and Kissinger watchers weren't at all surprised to see photographs of Henry ogling a mistress of that ancient terpsichorean art. When asked, Kissinger admits that moving into the top echelon of world figures has been responsible for a massive build-up in his confidence. "Especially my social confidence. It guarantees the success of a Washington dinner party if the host or hostess can entice me to go—and that is very flattering."

Photographers haunted Kissinger whenever he appeared socially in Washington and Gloria Steinem once said, "The trouble is that when a girl is photographed next to Henry Kissinger it is like a hunter standing with an elephant gun next to an elephant. They assume she is going big-game hunting."

Kissinger enjoyed the free talk about his swinging sex life and the show-business girls who made themselves available to him for publicity's sake. A reporter once asked him, "Which would you prefer, since something is going to be written about it, should I refer to it as your sex life or your social life?"

Kissinger chuckled and said, "I work up to eighteen hours a day in Washington. When I go out I want to enjoy myself. When I am out on the Coast at the White House in San Clemente, I have more free time. I enjoy the company of these girls. They are beautiful and I find some of them interesting. There isn't any more to it than that. It's not an emotional thing. They aren't going to want me to marry them."

Judy Brown is a phenomenon of the 1970's—a porn star or an actress in X-rated movies. It depends on which columnist you're reading and Miss Brown's mood of the moment. Standing five feet four, with brown eyes, dark hair, and enormous breasts whose proportions are dramatized by the gowns Judy prefers, Miss Brown arrived in Hollywood by the modern route.

A pretty girl with the right kind of "Sugar Daddy" back in Joan Crawford's day used to make it from *Miss Something or Other* to a stock contract in one fell swoop. Or if she preferred something better than the standard seventy-five dollar a week contract, there were the Hollywood drive-ins where delicious dolls encountered few problems in peddling their assets between hoisting trays.

Judy had been *Miss University of Missouri* but reached the film capital by way of Denmark where her considerable assets were peddled in a Danish film called *Threesome*. The United States Customs Service, that valiant custodian of public morals, chose to destroy the negative when it reached New York for distribution in America. Then, as has been happening since the late Bennet Cerf chose to make a test case of the ban on James Joyce's *Ulysses*, the Customs people reversed themselves. *Threesome* was seen in Judy's native land and enough was visible to find her steady work at Universal, one of the few lots left that carries contracts with young ladies.

Judy Brown had gone on to greater celluloid triumphs in *Women in Cages*, and *The Big Doll House* when she met Henry. It had been arranged as a blind date by a mutual friend. One can only speculate that Henry had spotted Judy during one of his eighteen-hour work days. Perhaps his interest in foreign relations had led him into a D.C.

porn house and *Threesome*.

Judy, who told all, but very all, in a number of signed movie magazine articles, confessed that she almost called the date off. "What on earth would I ever say to Henry Kissinger?" she asked herself.

Good question.

Whatever she said must have pleased Henry whose penchant for cleavage had grown ever more pronounced since his association with Jill St. John. They were spotted around Hollywood in the places where they were supposed to be spotted— to the joy of the lady's press agent.

From his vivid typewriter came a running account of what was blossoming into a romance so torrid that, if ever filmed, it would have to be shown on an asbestos screen. Judy made chopped liver for him and Henry reportedly told her, "You'd better stop that or I'll fall in love with you."

Obviously Henry had never tasted Golda Meir's chopped liver.

They went to the beach where they lay in the sun together—READING. Henry, the Hollywood press buzzed, read *The Godfather* and Judy wrapped herself in *The New Centurions*.

For the first time in his role of philanderer, Henry found himself boxed in. He began to worry about how dating a bosomy porn star would "play in Peoria." The Katzenjammer Kids, alas, had gotten to him.

Nevertheless he took Judy to dinner at *Le Bistro*, one of those intimate "eateries" of the Southland where celebrities enjoy about the same privacy a political candidate does at Nathan's in

Coney Island. No one needed Judy's press agent. Everyone who was anyone at *Le Bistro* got on the phone to columnists and photographers to tell them that Henry Kissinger was dining with GUESS WHO? That was Hollywood reciprocity at its most workmanlike. For their information the celebrities guaranteed themselves coverage for weeks ahead. A Henry Kissinger-Judy Brown photo was easily worth ten Robert Redfords with the same lady.

While Judy was powdering her nose, Secret Service agents told Henry that the street was filling up with reporters and photographers. Judy and her escort were bundled out the back entrance, steered through the kitchen by the management in the time-honored tradition of the film colony.

It was enough to warm old reporters' hearts. There hadn't been events like that around town since the days when Ava Gardner used to throw champagne glasses at photographers and slug taxi drivers over the head with her slipper.

As an exit line, Judy screamed, "If you're so ashamed to be seen with stars, why do you go out with them?"

As they tell it, loquacious, articulate Doctor Kissinger was able to summon a quick answer in two short words—one, of four letters, the other one was "you."

That was the end of the affair, and Golda Meir must have been dismayed by the recriminations that followed. Judy took to the public print with her account of the involvement, maintaining that it had been strong and wonderful, sentimental and beautiful—until that tragic night.

Judy summoned the press and said, "I've done everything in my power to play down our relationship, even to barefaced denials to specific questions about our dating. Henry has appreciated my discretion.

"But now I've had it. I've got an ego, too, and he's got to realize that it hurts my feelings to see him written about all over the place with other women. Especially when I know they don't mean anything to him, like Margaret Osmer, like Marlo Thomas. He went out with her too. He didn't even know what she did. She said she worked in television and he said 'What do you do?' like maybe she was a secretary. The next day their picture was plastered all over the newspapers. A million people are talking about Marlo Thomas and Henry Kissinger and that hurts. I'm tired of being the silent one in his life, the mystery girl."

Judy went on and on—into the fan magazines and more interviews in which she claimed that it had been a tempest in a tea pot, that Henry was just a little upset at *Le Bistro*. She predicted they'd be together again and Henry had promised her he'd sit still for photographers wherever she wanted—in restaurants, in her apartment (serving him chicken liver?) down at the beach reading *The Godfather*.

When asked about Judy and her claims of his loyalty, Henry clammed. "Not so. Not true at all." Why, he'd only been out with the girl three times, just for dinner."

Dr. Kissinger could get away with that kind of stuff in Washington with impunity but not in Hollywood, the smog-swept land of Joyce Haber and

Rona Barrett, heirs to the crowns of Louella Parsons and Hedda Hopper. The gossip columnists had done their homework. They came up with a list of the places Judy and Henry had been seen together—and quite a collection they were—Kissinger's digs in San Clemente, Judy's apartment in Beverly Hills, the usual restaurants, a sneaky side road hideout in Palm Springs. It was enough to make readers tingle.

The business of history making was on Henry's side and he darted away to China, one of those manufactured colds and rest cures high in the Himalayas and Judy stayed in Hollywood where she announced the color of her new nail polish as "Kissinger red."

A veteran Hollywood newspaperman, glancing at the mess of clippings he'd assembled for a feature on the Kissinger-Brown affair shook his head and sighed, "Can you imagine the stink there would have been twenty-five years ago if Henry Kissinger had been caught having cocktails with Ingrid Bergman on the Via Veneto when she was pregnant by Roberto Rosselini. They would have been calling for lifting of his naturalization papers in Congress, the way they wanted Bergman labelled an 'undesirable alien.' "

One of the troubles with an image is that it is hard to maintain—especially if the subject isn't all that cooperative. While Henry cherished his role of playboy and devoted many evening hours to it, he couldn't always satisfy the expectations of the news hounds.

They sought to tie him up with Marlo Thomas, actress-daughter of comedian Danny Thomas, a very serious young lady who does things for love and because she is interested in them. Marlo does not dedicate herself to the accumulation of money like, say, Kirk Douglas, or to jewels, like ZsaZsa Gabor. Yet both Marlo and Zsa Zsa were manufactured into Kissinger hobbies during his San Clemente-Hollywood perigrinations.

Marlo Thomas was reported jogging with Henry along the Pacific beach. Jogging strikes one as the sort of thing Marlo Thomas would do. But not Henry Kissinger. After the jogging story, the Marlo Thomas file was closed.

Zsa Zsa lasted a bit longer, long enough for Henry to promise he would be at the Las Vegas unveiling of her night club act. With a perspicacity that would have earned him the chair of Senior Officer of the New York Critics Circle, Henry arranged to be in Paris that night negotiating with "Ducky." He sent Zsa Zsa a dozen roses instead—gesture that did not markedly improve her performance.

Robert Evans, Paramount Studios president, at the time the husband of Ali McGraw, often fixed up Kissinger with a date with a starlet and one of them remarked, "That's something I could never understand. Henry doesn't need that sort of help. He could do all right on his own. But I guess he's afraid. He wants someone to lay the groundwork, so he doesn't always get taken advantage of. Friendship and power go awfully well together."

Kissinger once remarked, "Power is the ultimate aphrodisiac."

Sometimes Henry used his power benevolently. Actress Ruta Lee spent years begging various government agents to help her get her grandmother out of Siberia where they had been deported from Lithuania.

In 1971 a studio executive arranged for her to date Henry. It was broken but they finally met a year later. Henry helped Ruta get both her grandmother and aunt out of Siberia.

Kissinger, in time, began feeding gags to the media. After one of his vanishing acts he told reporters who questioned the official version. He said that he'd been in Acapulco for four days. "I've got four witnesses to prove it," he said, "all girls."

Henry grew adept at generating this kind of publicity when it counted. Once in Paris he was photographed emerging from a night club with CBS-TV producer Meg Osmer, the girl who got Judy Brown into such a tizzy. Two days later when he reported to Nixon and Secretary of State Rogers at San Clemente Rogers asked him, "Who was that woman?" Kissinger answered, "Oh, that must have been Mme. Binh"—the Viet Cong foreign minister—and the three men roared with laughter for the TV cameras. Later it turned out that he had in fact secretly met Mme. Binh and Hanoi's Le Duc Tho on that particular Paris trip.

Kissinger never really got down to the business of proclaiming an end to his involvement with the glamor ladies. It came step by step. He remained friends with Jill St. John who bitterly resented the insinuation in the gossip columns that she had become a female George Hamilton—currying

Henry, as George did Lynda Bird Johnson, because of her White House authority. Jill wanted it known that her relationship with Henry was based upon intellectual things, like discussing world events and playing chess. "I enjoy playing with Henry Kissinger much more than Sean Connery. I don't know why. He's just more fun to play with."

This mind-boggling information was relayed to a fan magazine writer by Miss St. John and somewhere in some trivia compendium it must be filed under the heading of "You have to be kidding, Jill."

Henry also saw a lot of Margaret Osmer who proved useful when he required a circumspect cover for one of his flights to nowhere. But one day, Henry appeared to be just a bit tired of it all. It was at a major Washington conference, an aide recalls. Henry stopped the discussion, leaned back in his chair and said, "It is astonishing, you know. These starlets, these actresses I go out with. They aren't even sexy."

Kissinger a skilled man at seeing all sides of an issue, didn't ask the follow-up question, what those movie starlets thought of him—and other big shot politicians who shared their beds? Someone might have told him.

Dorothea, at thirty-one-plus is a little too old to be a starlet, although she doesn't look her age. She's petite, blonde, with pink-white skin, bright blue eyes and a remarkable conversational range, at home with the latest books, the new styles, the youth thing, the Establishment—whatever you want Dotty can supply. Her private passion is opera. "My real name's Lucia," she said. "But

Italian girls are a dime a dozen in towns like this, so I thought I'd give them the WASP touch when I started getting around. It couldn't hurt. Something different."

Dotty has done her turn in the acting business —bit parts mostly and she keeps getting them because she's capable and popular. Her main job is entertaining men. "I don't smoke and I don't drink," she explained. "I've got a good reputation. I date only big timers. The agents and studio people who call me know this, so I've had my share of fellows like Kissinger." Dotty only smiles if you ask if she had ever dated Henry. "No comment," she says.

"They're no different from anyone else, just lonely guys with some time on their hands. They get sick and tired of all the restrictions. They want to get away, forget it, just drop into some out-of-the-way place and enjoy an evening with a girl who's not too dumb. And it doesn't pay to be bright either. They don't want that intellectual stuff at night.

"I think that Henry got himself a raw deal here in Hollywood. They played him for a sucker. One right after the other—grabbing all kinds of snide publicity. But, hell, it didn't harm him—and certainly, not them.

"I know how they feel. They can take their pick of what's available in Hollywood. The men run the place now more than ever. And they're plenty of them. Which is a change. But what they offer is the same old stuff—lots of talk about themselves, some quick action, a hundred, two hundred, maybe. Or they'll send you a shopping certificate.

Some really go to the trouble of picking out gifts —really nice, thoughtful things.

"But the Washington fellows—they're different. They've got power. You sometimes get to travel with them on the government planes. I've done that. All those Secret Service men around— it makes you feel important. I guess it means they give you a special kick. They're a novelty.

"I knew a gal who slept with a president. She's dead now. I won't mention his name. You can figure it out. I shouldn't say she just slept with him. It happened lots of times. She was a great gal— sober. He got a kick out of her. They say it's all coming out pretty soon in a new book about her.

"I don't know. Maybe it's just gossip. I only know what I know. She didn't keep a diary, but she made notes about the times she spent with him. She kept them with her jewelry in a safe deposit box. For a cooky gal she was pretty careful about things like that.

"Anyway when this president died, his family swooped down on her and every other gal he'd screwed in Hollywood—maybe, even in the country. They were backed up by Government agents—the F.B.I. maybe. I don't know. But she told me how they sweat it out of her—made her give up everything she had connected with him, autographed photos, the diary, a few little gifts that didn't mean a damn but could be identified. Those guys knew everything—more than she did.

"I remember once when I was a kid I met Marion Davies, the old-time movie star. Stoned out of her mind but a sweet, great woman, always doing something for charity. This was a party for youngsters. My old lady was a volunteer.

"She'd been the mistress of William Randolph Hearst for years. He was the big publisher, the grandfather of Patricia Hearst. They lived in a castle in San Simeon and during the Depression she hocked her jewels so he could hold on to his publishing interests.

"Old man Hearst died in her home in Beverly Hills. The family knew he was checking out. They saw to it that Marion got sloshed. Then they fed her sleeping pills to make sure she was out cold when Hearst died.

"When Marion woke up, there was no one there—just the servants. The Hearst sons and all their men had disappeared. They'd taken the old man's body with them, shipped it to San Francisco, and there it was for three days—lying in state in a big Cathedral for the thousands of people who lined up. Some of them said they wanted to make sure old Hearst was dead.

"The only one who never got to see him was Marion, the woman who loved him. Power can be one helluva thing, can't it? You wonder, sometimes, if a guy like Henry Kissinger ever comes down off his high and really thinks about it. Maybe not. Maybe he hasn't got the time. But for a woman—it's something to be a part of, to share even for a few minutes. It's worth a roll in the hay."

PART FOUR

After the Rise, the ?

"Henry praises only estimates of strength and force. If you do not have a nuclear bomb under your pillow, he is not interested. Look at the North Vietnamese, Indira Gandhi, the Japanese and me. Because we have no nuclear bomb under our pillow, Henry never expected our reaction."
—Danielle Hunebelle, French journalist.

CHAPTER FOUR

Perhaps in unconscious envy, perhaps because it was just more fun, the intrigued observers of Washington's most-watched "swinging bachelor" devoted much of their attention to the swinging— very little to the rest of his bachelorhood.

Until his marriage to Nancy Maginnes, Henry lived alone in an elegant, rented townhouse in Washington's embassy section, not far from Rock Creek Park. Whenever he entertained which was rarely, he asked one of his women friends to handle his parties for him at their homes. The few guests he invited to his house were generally there on business, and not expected to comment or be dismayed by the quality of Kissinger's housekeeping.

His household staff consisted of a cleaning woman who came in a couple of times a week, did superficial dusting and departed, leaving the rest of the mess for Henry to clean up or live with as he chose. French reporter Danielle Hunebelle, one of the few visitors, later wrote of the dirty laundry strewn in Henry's bedroom. Barbara Howar dubbed the decor, "early Holiday Inn."

"It was what I'd expect" Howar said, "of a bachelor who's been divorced, whose entire furnishings are all the things that fell off the moving van as the wife moved out."

Some things he shared with ordinary, working-stiff bachelors. One morning, while a pair of reporters waited outside to speak to him before he got into his White House limousine, Henry emerged carrying a huge bundle of dirty laundry and an armful of suits for the dry cleaner.

After the divorce of the Kissingers, their friends were faced with the unpleasant decision of choosing which friendship to maintain. Most have chosen to keep up with Henry.

Whatever bitterness existed at the end of their fifteen years of marriage has outwardly been dissipated and both parents unselfishly share their two children. They assemble as a family on holidays and appropriate occasions and Henry, now that he can communicate to Elizabeth and David, who are in their teens, has become a warmly affectionate father, vastly more patient in dealing with them than with his subordinates.

If bachelor Kissinger appeared more harried than usual in the last year of the Nixon administration as he shot into his car in the morning carrying an untidy collection of dirty clothes there were many reasons, some, private, deeply personal; others, larger, international, historic in scope. Kissinger was forced to summon all his intellect and mental resources to separate, analyze and consider the impact on his vast world of the Watergate scandal which was rapidly drawing to a crescendo.

"I believe," Henry Kissinger once said, "in the tragic element of history. I believe there is the tragedy of a man who works very hard and never gets what he wants. And then I believe there is the even more bitter tragedy of a man who finally gets what he wants and finds out that he doesn't want it." Kissinger discreetly failed to mention the third man, who works all his life to achieve a pinnacle of achievement and then fails miserably in fulfilling his ambitions because, in battling to the top, his own character became flawed. This would have been the parable of Henry's patron and friend, Richard Nixon.

In January, 1974 Henry Kissinger achieved his finest hour. He had wrapped up his historic Mideast agreement; now, with° a few close friends looking on, the new Secretary of State had come to the department's crowded auditorium to tell newsmen how he had done it.

But Kissinger barely got the chance. No sooner had the press conference begun than the triumphal atmosphere was tainted by Watergate—and Kissinger tinged. New suggestions that Kissinger might have committed perjury had been made in the Senate Foreign Relations Committee. Reporters hammered away at his role in the wiretapping of some of his National Security Council aides.

It became a devastating public affair and television audiences, for the first time, saw the man under awful pressure. His face reddened. His voice cracked, his fingers clenched. At one point he erupted, "This is a press conference and not a cross-examination."

In a sense, though, it was. Kissinger's trouble dated back to 1969 when the White House, furious over NSC leaks, reacted characteristically. It summoned the FBI to investigate and then plucked David Young, from Kissinger's own staff, to set up the super-secret "plumbers" investigative unit. Kissinger denied knowing Young's connection with the "plumbers" and declared that his role in the FBI probe had been limited to submitting names to J. Edgar Hoover of the seventeen staffers who had access to classified information. He maintained that he had never initiated any taps.

Kissinger's emotional display, the curtain-raiser to his Salzburg tearful resignation threat, raised eyebrows in the capital—and the caustic comment expected of hard-nosed politicians. Henry spent the evening with Senator Fulbright agonizing over the day's events and presumably Fulbright reassured him calmly that there existed the utmost confidence in his office and that he was expected to do nothing more than tell the truth. Fulbright undoubtedly also reminded Kissinger of Harry Truman's advice, "If you can't take the heat, stay out of the kitchen."

With reason, the press leaped on Kissinger after the conference which, on television at least, suggested a nervous Secretary of State caught in a bold lie. Kissinger's penchant for furtive, secret negotiations had caught up with him. Columnists, who once supported Henry, affording him a wide generous platform for his views, now lumped him with Ehrlichman and Haldeman, of whom Henry said, "They are men with a Gestapo mentality."

This was pretty rough stuff, especially when liberal columnist Shana Alexander wrote that Kissinger "had sunk from statesman to a mere footman at the throne of power." William White offered: "The build-up of Henry Kissinger, able and useful though he is, into a Kissinger that never was has now come to a jarring halt."

Kissinger was shocked by the sting of the criticism. The press he had cultivated assiduously turned on him as angrily as they had on the White House staffers they despised. Alexander Haig took to the telephone to try to persuade key columnists and political reporters to soften their tone—that the Administration was in enough boiling water and the country couldn't survive an attack from still another direction. "Some reporters," Haig said, "have a commitment to destroy; they're on a crusade."

Watergate posed enormous problems for Henry Kissinger, the man who had worked very hard to get what he wanted and knew exactly what to do with his position and his power now that he had gotten there. Separating himself from Watergate without breaking with Nixon personally was like walking on eggs and there had already been cracks produced by the secret bombing of Cambodia.

Critics of the Administration saw a parallel between the secret bombing and the secret operations of Watergate. They were denounced as equally wrong. Kissinger maintained that an action to save American lives could be secret and legal at the same time. This was not true of Watergate which he considered both illegal and stupid. Kissinger was harder pressed to validate the justification of bombing a neutral country. But because he was Kissinger—the super-statesman—he successfully managed to weather the storm. He represented the last link, somewhat tarnished perhaps, between the Nixon administration and what thoughtful Americans regarded as common decency.

Kissinger seriously thought of resigning. He was aware of his historical stature—no doubt of that. He had been an innovator, a revolutionary in foreign policy, a pragmatic diplomat, a wily European, who had shown Americans that more flexibility was needed in a modern world. That the era of self-righteousness represented by John Foster Dulles (who refused even to shake hands with the Chinese) had irrevocably been passed by time and circumstance.

He was damned if he did, damned if he didn't. To resign would lay Henry open to the accusation of deserting a sinking ship, public criticism would enlarge to where his patriotism would be questioned by the press and public. Kissinger, as a quitter, would be hanged in the public opinion polls.

Yet to remain under the shadow of Watergate would cloud his own future. But that could wait. On a more immediate level Kissinger worried that if the United States continued to be consumed by Watergate it would automatically forfeit its right to restore peace to the world. He felt that Watergate was undermining his own efforts and, in time, all the authority he had nurtured would be dissipated.

Kissinger turned to his friends and the nights grew longer and longer as they pondered the options. Henry talked to Haig, to Rockefeller, other men he trusted for advice. Some wanted him to resign, seeing the defection of the Administration's Senior Officer as the quickest route to Richard Nixon's abdication. Others, like Haig, described a Kissinger resignation as the equivalent of desertion in wartime.

The ground plan was being laid for the strategy of the Five Days in August when Kissinger, Haig and St. Clair artfully maneuvered Nixon into quitting. Nixon, in one of his artless attempts to distract public attention from Watergate, turned to a move that had too long been postponed, naming Henry Kissinger Secretary of State.

William Rogers had wanted "out" for a long time. His old friendship with Richard Nixon, their law firm partnership, would haunt him the rest of his life. He had been the most innocuous figure an innocuous Administration, until it became dangerous, a bridge-playing traveller who performed minor Foggy Bottom functions while Kissinger functioned dramatically and spectacularly on the world scene. Rogers owned the title; Kissinger possessed the power.

Rogers wanted neither, really, but he had hung around the capital out of perverse loyalty to Nixon. Or was that the reason? Since so little was heard from Rogers while he headed the Nixon cabinet he emerges as one of its most fascinating "mystery guests." His memoirs ought to be worth triple the two million asked by Richard Nixon.

Whatever the motives behind Kissinger's nomination, the diplomat accepted them, remaining true to his pragmatism. "It tied me to the job," he told intimates and it eliminated the necessity for a private decision. The Kissinger men recognized that it was a Nixon ploy, another move to forestall his resignation. But that was only a matter of time as Kissinger reminded himself when he said, "History won't wait for us to sort ourselves out."

President Nixon announced Kissinger's nomination at San Clemente, expecting, of course, that it was of sufficient note to sidetrack Watergate questions. It wasn't. The reporters jotted it down and doggedly phrased and rephrased the questions they had asked so many times in the year past, the same questions Nixon dodged with increasingly nervous apprehension. The sweat stood out on his brow. His hands trembled. The smile became even more forced. In many ways, it was pathetic, but newsmen, so accustomed to the man's evasions, barely noticed. They were witnessing just another Nixon charade.

By contrast, the first appearance of Henry Kissinger before the press corps on the following morning was almost joyous. A sort of love-feast between men who had come to admire and respect him—even in attack. Henry appeared relaxed and comfortable. When he was asked about how his "family heritage" might affect U.S. policy in the Middle East, Kissinger replied, "I am asked to conduct the foreign policy of the United States, and I will conduct the foreign policy of the United States regardless of religious and national heri tage. There is no other country in the world in which a man of my background could be considered for an office such as the one for which I have been nominated, and that imposes on me a very grave responsibility which I will pursue in the national interest."

At the end of the conference a reporter, gingerly posed what he called a "technical question." "Do you prefer to be called Mr. Secretary or Dr. Secretary."

Kissinger didn't miss a beat. "I don't stand on protocol," he replied, smiling, "If you just call me Excellency, it will be okay."

That was worth a Gold Star on any reporter's notebook. The secret swinger had kept the faith. This was the old, relaxed, sneaky, fascinating Kissinger, the mystery man who, in the main, had kept his cool while the rest of the Nixon Administration was tumbling down a wall at a time.

He was like a breath of fresh air in a capital whose moral pollution had become as devastating as that in the atmosphere.

Unlike the parents of the bride who do not lose a daughter but gain a son, America gained a new Secretary of State but lost its favorite playboy. Nancy Maginnes, who had been hovering in the wings, was about to make her entrance and Kissinger's boudoir antics would be relegated to footnotes of history.

While they lasted, they were great good fun, and the most pleasant part was the obvious relish with which the American people accepted the Kissinger image. He'd managed what few politicians had ever accomplished in this country—leading an outrageous private life without losing respect. The voters seemed to feel that in view of his accomplishments he deserved whatever kicks he could get, and if a man with his looks needed to rely on his job to get a date, so what?

After his experience with Judy Brown, Henry learned to avoid the actresses who used him for publicity. He dated Sammantha Eggar, Joanna Barnes, Hope Lang, Candy Bergen and the eternal June Wilkinson. Their names didn't exactly avoid being coupled with Henry's, but his friends had the feeling that these girls dated him because they were intrigued—that they wanted their own private answer to the question on so many feminine minds, "What is Henry Kissinger really like?"

Barbara Howar offered a few clues about Kissinger's attitude toward women. She said, "Henry likes women. Conversation with them is not tiring; they neither bore nor challenge him. Nixon and Kissinger are alike in their squareness; both are puritanical and moral men who believe a woman's place is three paces behind the politician. She is little more than a good wife, mother, friend, never the 'shrewd little sounding board' that Democratics patronizingly termed their woman. They are docile little followers."

Unlike Miss Brown who finally broke down and admitted she could understand why Henry beat a hasty exit from *Le Bistro* when the next day's papers contained an announcement of Henry's visit to China, Barbara found mixed blessings in the coupling of her name with Henry's. It affected her career as a Washington commentator.

"For every public linking of my name with Henry's," Barbara wrote, "there were disproportionate benefits. He was wont to boast that he did more to advance the woman's movement than any public official. To some extent, that was so, for an accessibility to Henry Kissinger gave a woman leverage within the male power structure of whatever publication or television medium she worked in. I could be disrespectful of Nixon, as opposed to the war as a Buddhist priest and as disdainful of the Establishment on the air as I wanted to be as long as there were photographs of me with Henry in magazines and reports in the newspapers of being seen with him."

Miss Howar further complained, "For all the rewards in associating with Henry, all the commercial spoils of being 'in' with power, there were for me an increasing number of public incidents more annoying than gratifying. Being constantly asked about Dr. Kissinger was not everything I could desire. Magazine interviewers inevitably got around to the question: 'Now, tell me, what is Henry Kissinger *really* like?'"

There was one gal who *really* had the answer— or so she said. She was Danielle Hunebelle, a respected French journalist with what have been described as "gamine good looks" who came to Washington for an interview for the distinguished French magazine, *Realites* and to do a television film on Kissinger. No newspaper man or woman could have summoned more impeccable credentials than Miss Hunebelle. Her magazine is an international powerhouse and government-controlled television, to the dismay of French listeners, is as conservative and circumspect as the man who molded it into his own image, Charles De Gaulle. Expecting Miss Hunebelle to go ape over Henry Kissinger amounts in predictability to discover Walter Lippmann° coming out of retirement to take up with Judy Brown.

But, a funny thing happened on the way to the White House.

In kind moments, those involved in *l'affaire Hunebelle* appear to feel that Danielle didn't quite understand Henry's flirtatious ways. For instance, he has been known to greet lady journalists with, "When are the two of us going to get together?" or "Those hot pants are certainly something. You know I like hot pants very much. Especially those hot pants. What are you trying to do? Seduce me?"

Any American girl would have realized that passes in language like that haven't been made since the Twenties when Dorothy Parker wrote, "Men don't make passes at girls who wear glasses."

Danielle, misunderstanding Henry's way with the language, evidently took him seriously, for she fell completely under his spell. They did the interviews, but a relationship that should have ended there didn't. "Henry had no one to blame but himself," said a friend. "He was a damned fool, but hasn't he always been about pretty young women? The French woman began writing him mad letters—love letters telling him how he had fired up her passions and that she couldn't live without him. She was a writer, all right. Then she began peppering his office with telephone calls. Any sensible man would have picked up the phone and told her to get lost. Any sensible man in his position would have had her visa revoked. But Henry didn't. He chose to let the whole thing slide. That's what he thought. It only got worse."

When he went to Paris after Danielle finally had returned there he spent a night out on the town with Margaret Osmer. Depressed at not seeing Henry—and jealous—Danielle ran her car off the road in what the newspapers described as a "suicide attempt" because of her unrequited love for Henry Kissinger. Publishing became a joy for Europe's scandal press, as from one end of the continent to the other, they seized on the story, tossing it around like a wondrous toy balloon. Not since the days of Elizabeth Taylor and Richard Burton and their odyssey down the Nile in "Cleopatra" had there been such an uproar. But that was only the beginning. Henry had not heard the last of Danielle.

She was not a newspaperwoman for nothing. Danielle holed up in her Paris apartment and deftly turned out a book called *Dear Henry* in which she poured out her feelings for the American diplomatic genius. It was the frenzied prose of a *woman scorned* as with total disgust she described Henry's disorderly bedroom as full of filthy laundry. She let her readers know that Henry's table manners were disgusting, his hands pudgy, his fingers, thick and ugly. She described their passions, saying "We were two romantics, made for the heights of love, like Tristan and Isolde."

Even the book's publication, the sort of denouement that usually terminates bizarre relationships like that of Danielle and Henry, failed to soften the lady's wrath. When she heard of Henry's dismay at the book and his surprise that she had turned on him so violently, Danielle snapped, "Henry praises only estimates of strength and force. If you do not have a nuclear bomb under your pillow, he is not interested. Look at the North Vietnamese, Indira Gandhi, the Japanese and me. Because we have no nuclear bomb under our pillow, Henry never expected our reaction."

Time will tell whether *Dear Henry* will make a repertorial star out of Danielle, but it is pretty safe to assume that she will have a difficult time being welcomed back to the United States if she intends taking on Washington again. The State Department, which issues visas, is one of those bureaucracies with long memories that live from Administration to Administration and has been collecting lists of "nasty people" for years and years.

Writers, especially, are subject to closer scrutiny than most visitors to our shores. Even American journalists who list "writer" as a convenient explanation of their profession, wait nervously in the passport control line while an Immigration flunky thumbs through a thick dossier of "undesirables" to seek out their names. That the fellow passed through a few seconds earlier may have been a bank robber and been accorded a "welcome home" doubles the irritation.

Henry eventually was able to lose Danielle and once told a visitor, "If you speak to me three times, our relationship will be deeper than mine was with Hunebelle." When Nora Ephron, one of the country's top magazine writers, asked a Kissinger aide if she might see his boss for longer than she'd been promised, he looked up, "Another Hunebelle?"

When you stop to think about it, in the few years Henry worked at the Casanova business, he did an extraordinary job. For a man who worked sixteen hours a day (his own claim) and had only eight hours to pack in the nocturnal divertisements he managed not only to get to know an amazing number of young women, but successfully divided them into two stables. And except for the Judy Brown outburst against Ms. Thomas and Ms. Osmer, he successfully kept them at bay and at peace. Perhaps, in his diplomatic wanderings, he had uncovered some of the secrets by which Arab sheiks maintained their harems over the centuries.

Most of the known ladies in Henry's little black book have appeared on these pages. To divide them into camps, Misses Brown, Miss Love Bunny and others represented the Playboy Bunny image —the friend of man type who, after dinner, would rub Henry's neck and back. The others belonged to Henry's official world—ladies who graced his arm when the prize bachelor needed someone to accompany him to a diplomatic gathering or to show the public, now and then, that he wasn't really quite the swinger the press made him out to be.

In alphabetical order, they were Barbara Howar, Nancy Maginnes, Gloria Steinem, early in the swinging era, and Barbara Walters. Gallantly Kissinger would rate them all equals in his book of records, but the press maintained its own private scratch sheet. Gloria, they knew, couldn't last long around Henry. She was too opinionated and the leader of Women's Lib certainly wouldn't walk three paces behind any Secretary of State. Barbara Howar appeared to be telling the truth when she complained that association with Henry was more of a professional burden than an asset. Divorced Barbara Walters needed neither Henry Kissinger or Richard Nixon on her arm nearly as much as they needed her. The first lady of television was a powerhouse in her own right, a fact of which she was fully aware. Beneath that gentle voice there bleeds a heart of granite.

Quite clearly Henry was one of the men Barbara could associate with and have it recognized as purely an intellectual evening, not a dalliance. That is something Barbara has assiduously avoided in her public image as the greatest purveyor of serious thought and culture to American women since Kate Smith's daily news program of radio fame.

Unlike Kate, who ended with Kate Smith's *Thought For The Day*, preceded and closed with a fanfare, Miss Walters caters to a generous, sophisticated public and old-fashioned "playing around" would not affect her position in the least. Times have changed. However Barbara, for the moment at least, prefers keeping her cool on and off the tube.

All along, the oddsmakers were laying their bets on Nancy Maginnes as the gal who'd eventually cook breakfast for Henry—long before "breakfast cooking" became the "in" American thing. Beneath that stern, uncompromising, grim-faced, cold calculating heart of Henry Kissinger, grizzled, cynical, stern, shrewd newspaperman knew there beat a heart of pure mush—exactly like their own. Get a newspaperman drunk and you'll meet a sentimental slob. Get a politician drunk, and you'll meet another sentimental slob. Henry Kissinger had not been marked by destiny to be the exception.

Reporters had seen the fates at work. Nancy was the gal he turned to in the big crises. She could be depended upon when their own instincts told the Kissinger watch that he needed her. What was astonishing about Nancy was that she didn't make a big thing out of it. The relationship blossomed of its own necessity. With necessity it acquired strength.

An old Washington reporter put it this way, "There was nothing so very different about Henry's swinging image. There have been lots of men around town like this, maybe not so high up the ladder perhaps, but big men in town. Once they escaped from an unhappy marriage they were just like a bunch of kids. What else could they be? They never had anything much in their lives—except politics and whatever kind of home their wives made for them.

"So they kicked over the traces. They dug chorus girls and strippers—kids like that. And why not? They have plenty to offer. Maybe a lot more than just being temporary wife or mother substitutes. The difference with Henry was that he got such a public kick out of it. There he was—an ugly big shot brain—sitting around with Nixon, Ehrlichman and Haldeman, trying to be brainy when what was really on his brains was bosoms. So he tried out bosoms. He liked it. And that was that.

"But it was in the cards that one day he'd kick over the traces. When a guy gets over the hump of fifty he forgets about the other one. His hands get tired of feeling so many different knees. He wants to settle down, especially if he was married a long time—like Kissinger. Too often, though, a guy picks out a dog for his second wife. Henry didn't. Nancy's great—but awfully 'new breed'—if you know what I mean. But Joe Alsop said it all when he quit newspapering, calling it 'a young man's game.' He's right. It's time for the Pat Nixons, the Lady Birds, the Mrs. Humphreys to call it quits too. Whatever happens to him from here on in, Henry's got it made with Nancy. He's one guy in the Nixon Washington who's come out smelling like roses. Not prize-winners, maybe, but good enough."

The American public, whose good-humored acceptance of the free-wheeling private life of Henry Kissinger and admiration of his diplomatic skills were largely responsible for his unique status as Super-Secretary of State, knew lots more about Judy Brown and Jill St. John than Nancy Maginnes. When Nancy and Henry slipped away to get married and headed for a honeymoon in Acapulco, the press chased after them.

The bride and groom good-naturedly gave up some of their privacy; Henry, to tell a few jokes; Nancy, to explain why their three-year engagement had lasted so long.

There was nothing impulsive, across-a-crowded-room about this romance between an Establishment, all-advantages, Episcopalian lawyer's daughter and the son of a German-Jewish immigrant, Nancy told the press, "It just grew. It takes time for two people to get close to each other. Everybody knows how old I am. I waited a long time to marry, but this was the right time for me."

Henry explained that he considered the marriage ceremony his *Bar Mitzvah* and had said in a toast at a family party, "All of you Episcopalians who have been picking on me so long, I want you to know that if I had my way we would have been married three years ago."

When Nancy Kissinger was asked about her husband's well-publicized activities as a bachelor and was his reputation as a ladies' man deserved, Nancy simply threw back her head and laughed—and laughed. Her reaction underscored the skepticism about the Secretary of State's carefully cultivated image as the playboy of the Nixon Administration and "secret swinger." Even then a close friend suspected that Kissinger's pleasure in such goings-on was cerebral rather than earthy. When it was suggested that he was probably a "secret non-swinger," he replied, "Don't tell anybody but you're right."

The marriage provoked not only newspaper features—notable for their friendly tone and good wishes for the couple—but editorial comment as well. On the CBS Evening News Eric Sevareid went on the air to say: "Traditionally, there were two kinds of official wives here: those from New York or Boston or Europe, who thought they were in a cultural Siberia and pined for the theatre and Bergdorf Goodman (Jacqueline Kennedy was one such); the other kind, who came from small towns, were bewildered and frightened and longed for home and the sewing circle—there are very few of those any more. Nancy Maginnes Kissinger is the prototype of the new breed: bright, highly educated, fashionable when she chooses to be, confident so that she doesn't need to see and be seen."

The public got a good look at Nancy during the protracted negotiations in the Middle East when she was photographed day after day at Kissinger's side while he made his ferryboat-style excursions between the capitals of the troubled countries. She didn't crunch down as to appear the same height as her husband and gave the impression of someone who tried to look her best in public—but didn't care too much if she goofed once in a while. There seemed nothing artificial or phony about her. Nancy's naturalness came over beautifully.

His marriage to Nancy Maginnes proved what Kissinger had been saying right along, "I go out with those actresses because I'm not very apt to marry one."

The mature woman he did marry has come to be known as the Greta Garbo of Cabinet wives, an aloof presence—or even better, if she can manage it, an aloof absence.

Aloofness, however, doesn't mean that she's chilly, distant or icy, she's one of the "new breed." As Sevareid mentioned, an independent and intellectual woman who undoubtedly floated her engagement for so long to make sure she wouldn't lose the things that interested her.

Nancy Kissinger, by her own account, spent most of her life in the company of men who took her intellectual capacities seriously and who did not regard her as a "little girl who would only paint flowers." She evidently wanted to make sure that his would not be the situation when she came to Washington as a Cabinet wife. Nancy clearly had no intention of joining the cocktail and canape set on any terms but her own.

She speaks admiringly of her employer of many years, Nelson Rockefeller, as one of the men who treated her as an intellectual equal. She was the only girl in a family of two brothers and numerous male cousins. Her father and most of her relatives were keenly interested in history and philosophy even if they were not involved professionally in these fields.

"I never had any sense of not being treated intellectually the same as my brothers," she said. "If I'd been one of those adorable cute little girls, maybe I'd have been treated like one."

The picture that emerges is of a husband ready to encourage his wife's intellectual interests and to respect her as a woman with her own mind, a lady who lived a great many years without him and might have continued to do so without noticeable anguish. Nancy, for her part, supplies a lot of what's been missing in Henry's life—steady companionship and someone to come home to. Both Kissingers give the impression of mature people who enjoy each other enormously and, as mature people, respect the other's individuality.

A part of Henry's life Nancy refused to have anything to do with was the quarters he'd been living in before their marriage. They stayed there briefly until Nancy found a more suitable house in Alexandria, Virginia. But it was hard going at the beginning as Henry's bachelor life style became exposed. Said Nancy, "There was nothing there you needed. You wanted to press a skirt? Well, there was no ironing board. Would you believe it? And no iron. And no emery boards. No scissors. You opened the drawer where the scissors were supposed to be and it wasn't there. He didn't even have a safety pin."

Nancy Kissinger is the kind of top drawer woman who doesn't come on strong—and that's refreshing. But neither does she retire, retreat, equivocate or avoid. A question gets an answer, and the answer can be depended upon to be serious and thoughtful. She's an intellectual and it was inevitable that she would be attracted to a man of Kissinger's dimensions. Of her husband Nancy says, "He has an excellent mind. He can't chat at the dinner table about his negotiations that day. It's classified and who wants to bring home his work? But we can and do discuss the history that led to negotiations." Conversation clearly is a staple commodity around the Kissinger home.

In his wife's view Henry is a warm, almost ebullient man with an enormous interest in other people. She finds that he talks with animated curiosity to foreign ministers and gardeners alike. "Whatever you say to him," Nancy notes, "he finds it important. I know that some people find Henry arrogant; they say that he is an egomaniac. Well, he does have a great deal of self-confidence, but you can always disagree with him. He will listen to you, as long as you have a knowledge of where you want to go. I don't think you could disagree with a real egomaniac."

Since Henry's marriage his name has disappeared from the gossip columns and for all you would know from reading the scandal tabloids there had never been any such person as the Super-Secretary Swinger.

The last prurient note appeared in one of the "new breed" Gay publications which reported—somewhat plaintively—that things weren't what they used to be along the roads and back lanes surrounding the property recently acquired by the Kissingers in Alexandria. The paper reported that the area used to be "great for cruising"—sort of a legal no man's land where Gays could search out their companions without interference from the police.

The Kissingers changed all that. The Secret Service came in, beefed up security precautions in all directions and now the area is patrolled constantly by official surveillance of one sort or another. The Gays have moved out.

Whether that dismayed the Secretary of State who struck such a blow for sexual freedom in antiseptic Washington hasn't been recorded.

Shortly after Gerald Ford took office as President he placed his arms around Henry Kissinger and told a startled assemblage of world statesmen, at the United Nations, "It should be emphatically understood that the Secretary of State has my full support and the unquestioned support of the American people." We have seen that Ford made his first move toward Kissinger within hours of being told of Richard Nixon's resignation. That Kissinger would remain as his senior Cabinet member became his first official announcement.

There were sound reasons for the move. Kissinger represented a vital link between the United States and the rest of the world. He was the only international figure the new Administration could lay its hands on and hold up as a symbol of the continuity of government. Once more Henry Kissinger had found a patron.

Only a few months before the Secretary of State was being acclaimed as one of the country's greatest national resources. After he returned from thirty-three days of Mid-East shuttle diplomacy with a disengagement agreement between Israel and Syria, *Newsweek* magazine pictured him on its cover on June 10, 1974 in a pop-art *Superman* suit with the letter "K" emblazoned on his chest.

President Ford's quick decision to retain the advice and wisdom of Henry Kissinger won universal applause. There were only a few doubting voices. One was Anthony Lake, a former member of Henry Kissinger's staff, presumably among the able men whose telephone had been bugged.

Wrote Lake: "Americans like most people need

heroes, and the more unheroic the times the more determined becomes the search for symbols of our greatness and even decency . . . Richard Nixon may never have seemed the model of a charismatic leader, but his elections and office conferred on him a quality of appearing larger than life.

"With his humiliation and resignation, American hope inclines all the more to a new symbol, Secretary of State Kissinger, as well as to such diverse figures as President Ford, Judge John J. Sirica, Senator Sam J. Ervin and the most attractive members of the House Judiciary Committee.

". . . The dangers of this situation are four-fold:

"First, such personal adulation to either a President or one of his Cabinet officers distorts needed debate about foreign policy . . .

"Second, the greater the hero worship, the shriller the critics sound will become. Frustrated by the uncritical acclaim for him from so many quarters, those who still speak out can fall into the trap of appearing to make unfair, sweeping assaults on his character and even competence. Up against hero worship, legitimate criticism begins to sound like ungrateful grousing. Debate, again, suffers.

"Third, Mr. Kissinger himself has helped create a situation in which he must be taken on an all-or-nothing basis. In today's Washington you are seen as for Mr. Kissinger or against him. No in-between . . .

"Finally, there is the problem of institutionalizing Mr. Kissinger's policies within the bureaucracy. The more that the man rather than his policies, attracts attention, the greater the possibility that his success will last only so long as he is in office."

The sniping did not take long to start and second thoughts about Super-Secretary Kissinger began to be found in the Pentagon, the White House and among the usual anonymous sources so dear to newspapermen. Stan Carter of the *New York Daily News* commented on a new controversy swirling around Henry Kissinger: "Reports have spread that the new President was considering removing Kissinger from his dual White House job as presidential advisor for national security affairs.

"Kissinger has continued to hold this post since becoming Secretary of State a year ago, giving him ready access to the President's Oval Office and prominence over the Defense Department and other agencies concerned with the making and carrying out of foreign policy. It is this 'second hat' that has made him a Super-Secretary with more power than any Secretary of State in history."

Carter pointed out that several senators sharply criticized Kissinger for, among other things, his role as head of the secret White House Committee of 40 in approving alleged covert activities by the Central Intelligence Agency to "destabilize" the Marxist regime in Chile before President Salvador Allende's overthrow and death a year ago.

Kissinger's enemies are also taking second looks at Kissinger because of his hope to keep military aid flowing to Turkey. Congress showed its new interest in participating in foreign policy by turning down President Ford's requests for military aid to Chile, fertilizer shipments to South Vietnam and it continued its scrutiny of further military aid to Turkey.

Thomas L. Hughes, a former director of the State Department's Intelligence Bureau, now president of the Carnegie Endowment for International Peace wrote: "We have made . . . an exceptional overinvestment in one exceptional man —Henry Kissinger—who has made some uncertain gains of uncertain desirability. In the process our national priorities have perforce become his preferences. Our national interests have become whatever he has time for at the moment."

Representative Albert Quie, one of Ford's oldest and closest friends and most frequently consulted advisors, openly called for Kissinger's resignation on the grounds of declining credibility.

As if realizing Kissinger was on the spot, the Senate finally got around to releasing Henry Kissinger's secret testimony about the bugging of his aides—the skeleton in Henry's closet that aroused more controversy than all the secrecy of his negotiations in Southeast Asia, China and the Middle East combined.

Wire-tapping was something Congress had come to expect from Richard Nixon. Back door negotiations had to be respected in foreign affairs. So they tolerated Kissinger's passion for secrecy. But bugging a man's own staff, on the curious grounds of press leaks, was the kind of practice his friends—and even his enemies—considered below Kissinger's intellectual dignity. "A man who had so little confidence in the top people around him shouldn't have appointed them in the first place" was how one State Department official put it.

The secret testimony Henry gave the Senate a few weeks before Nixon's resignation resurrected an old scapegoat, J. Edgar Hoover. Kissinger told a Senate panel that J. Edgar scorned him as a "Kennedy-type Harvard professor" and that he (Hoover) tapped the phones of three aides Kissinger had hired in spite of Hoover's displeasure.

In essence, Kissinger said Hoover alone had singled out three Kissinger aides as "security risks" and ordered their phones tapped as part of a 1969 drive by the White House "plumbers" to plug leaks of national security information.

This was because Kissinger ignored Hoover's advice not to hire the three men (whose names were deleted from the released testimony). Kissinger denied that he had ever consented to taps on his aides and that at a White House meeting when the subject came up he arrived late and the issue of wiretapping had already been decided.

Kissinger acknowledged that the first three aides to be bugged had been closely linked with the John Kennedy Administration. He said, "There is no doubt that some of my colleagues in the White House were very upset about the fact that I alone, of the senior officials in the White House, brought on my staff individuals who had been identified with the previous administration, with two of the previous administrations. There is also no doubt that the admiration of Mr. Hoover for the Kennedy family was very limited."

Kissinger said Hoover would never have taken

orders from him on who to wiretap "especially as I believe I also fitted some of the categories he considered invidious."

The testimony suggested the Senate panel members sympathized with Kissinger and regretted the need to investigate the allegations against him.

Said Hugh Scott, the old Nixon apologist from Pennsylvania, "This whole performance belongs in the Doonesbury cartoons rather than in the Senate Foreign Relations Committee."

It was a self-serving statement—sweeping aside with a quick joke a very real evil that had grown out of the Nixon years—the simple fact that no one believes anything any more that comes out of anybody in Washington.

Three years ago, even two years ago, with the whole Watergate mess started, you could have convinced even hard hats and hard liners that in his old age J. Edgar Hoover had been an old, senile fool. All you had to do was to shake your head and say, "He was a great patriot in his day BUT—" and there would be little disagreement.

But now the "SOB" is dead and it's an old, old tradition in politics that you can't lay the blame on a corpse. No one who's ever tried has gotten away with it. It didn't help Kissinger's image in the Gerald Ford "open door" Administration that the release of his testimony identifying J. Edgar Hoover as the bogeyman in his private Watergate coincided with reports increasingly identifying Secretary of State Kissinger as the major architect of supersecrecy in the conduct of U.S. foreign policy that allowed Washington to sponsor a hidden war against a democratically elected government in Chile even while our high officials were piously disclaiming any interventionist role.

An editorial in the *New York Daily News*, a paper normally friendly to containment of anything tinged with Communism, as certainly the Allende regime was; read: "As long as there is no full, free debate in which he openly participates, the impression will grow that Kissinger views himself as a special breed of public figure answerable neither to Congress nor the public and the press.

"In the aftermath of Watergate, no high official can long sustain that posture and command national confidence."

Wrote Anthony Lewis in the *New York Times:* "While opposing intervention in behalf of freedom in the Soviet Union, we now know, Mr. Kissinger presided over a program of subversion that helped turn Chile from democracy to tyranny. He did so not with his public attitude of concern for American values and respect for national sovereignty but with an arrogant assumption of the right to determine other societies. He reportedly told the Forty Committee which controls secret activities abroad, 'I don't see why we need to stand by and watch a country go Communist due to the irresponsibility of its own people.'

"There is no visible political substitute for Secretary Kissinger. But other institutions, in Congress and the Executive, must assert other values and other interests than his. We cannot let Mr. Kissinger alone define America's genius and the world's concerns."

Today's problems are vastly more complex,

more disorderly and more threatening than those existing when Kissinger stood at Mr. Nixon's side and promised to tell the President what he really should know—not what he wanted to know. So nimble Henry has slipped into a new role for him —that of economics advisor. No longer the high-minded optimist but the Prophet of Doom, Kissinger, both in Washington and the United Nations, is defining the woes of the world in the most solemn and apocalyptic terms. He maintains that democracy as we have known it in this century cannot survive for more than three or four years at the present rate of inflation.

If the people, parties and governments of the Free World do not cooperate and sacrifice to get this inflation under control, he says, the result will be anarchy, financial, economic and political. Authoritarian governments of the right and left will take over and Western civilization will be transformed into dictatorships.

Obviously Kissinger's pessimistic vision of the world of tomorrow, like all his views, is born of strong historical precedent. It is not simply a Dr. Strangelove theory—brewed to suit the personal needs of Henry Kissinger, a new platform from which to exercise his present power and collect more.

The trouble with it is that it just seems that way. Somehow, now that the Nixonites are gone— and their odor lingers on in the pardon, the trials and the San Clemente Elba of Richard Nixon— Kissinger doesn't quite appear as indispensable as in the first hours of the Ford Presidency. He reminds Americans of too many shabby tricks and diplomatic double dealing—Cambodia, the China journeys which appear now to have been Nixon-style window dressing, *detente* which is nowhere near *detente*—even if Americans added a new word, learned to spell it and pronounce its more or less correctly.

Then, there's the J. Edgar business—walking over the grave. And Chile? The all-American hard hat, the *his-country-right-or-wrong* type of *fella* might grant that Kissinger was doing "what's best for the country"—even if not quite sure of the exact geographical location of Chile. But the way he did it? And him really a foreigner? "Well, that stinks. Why don't they get rid of the guy?"

Even if he has been called indispensable, Kissinger really never had a sinecure on his jobs. His own worst enemy remained himself. Curiously, his strength lay in the support he enjoyed from Richard Nixon—and the contrast the public could see between the two men. For all his arrogance and ego there was the general feeling Kissinger genuinely was serving his country whereas Nixon was tending his own political and private interests.

Without Nixon, Kissinger stands revealed—naked as a jaybird with all his frailties, his immense intellect exposed as being the property of a man whose own character is as flawed as that of his former boss. All the warts have come out—the ego, the passion for secrecy, the somewhat childish delight in splash and spectacle, the weeper.

On the other side of the coin a politician has to be someone very special when Marvin and Bernard Kalb, skilled reporters, sit down and seriously describe him as "A Lancelot among the Brigands."

Even George Washington would have relished that description.

There is no doubt that Secretary of State Kissinger has become a global superstar, with the kind of international attraction rivaled only by a combination of Charles A. Lindbergh, the Prince of Wales and Marilyn Monroe. A comet of these dimensions does not fall to earth and snuff out on contact with the atmosphere.

Kissinger is only fifty-one. At this writing he does not appear to represent the kind of politician the country wants or even needs—regardless of his own opinion of his skills and his confidence in his predictions. Americans are worn down and beaten, weary of the old faces, the old liars. Kissinger's light burned brightest when it was concealing the darkness of the Nixon era. The more one sees it today, the more discernible become its flickers.

It will wane—and fade away—but not go out.

Like the Phoenix bird from the ashes it will rise, flutter and soar again. Kissinger may not be indispensable but there is an indestructible quality about him that will compel him to persist in pursuing his philosophy and drawing the people's attention. They admire Henry—and some day they may trust him.

As an old Hollywood admirer said, "He's got more comebacks in him than Frank Sinatra."

But will the world ever really know him? Probably not.

In the famous interview with Oriana Fallaci,

the Italian writer, which quoted Kissinger as describing himself as a "lone cowboy riding into town at high noon," Miss Fallaci complained that she had never interviewed anyone who "defended themselves as strenuously as you from attempts to penetrate their personality." Miss Fallaci asked, "Are you shy, by any chance, Dr. Kissinger?"

He answered yes, and no. He said both the mysterious, tormented image of him and the merry one were untrue. "I'm neither the one nor the other . . I'm . . . No, I won't tell you what I am. I'll never tell anyone."

And he hasn't.

THE NEWS TWISTERS
by Edith Efron with Clytia Chambers

A powerfully documented analysis that explodes the myth of network neutrality in reporting the news. It demonstrates and delineates how CBS, NBC, and ABC slanted and twisted the news against Richard Nixon during the 1968 presidential campaign. All shades of political opinion agree that this book is a must-read blockbuster!

"Explosive . . . a prodigious achievement!"—*William F. Buckley*

"A fantastic, shocking book!"—*The New Left Press*

"A vitally important book which every citizen should read!"—*Allen Drury*

12133—$1.25

HOW CBS TRIED TO KILL A BOOK
by Edith Efron with Clytia Chambers

The disturbing, at times terrifying story of the well-calculated public relations campaign launched by CBS News against THE NEWS TWISTERS and its findings of racial and political bias in network news.

"A broadside on bias!"—*Christian Science Monitor*

"This is a very shocking book!"—*Book News*

"Edith Efron is the Ralph Nader of broadcasting!"—*William F. Buckley*

15115—$1.50

THE AUTOBIOGRAPHY OF ISRAEL'S TOP AGENT

THE CHAMPAGNE SPY
EGYPT
by Wolfgang Lotz

Wolfgang Lotz was friend and confidant to Egyptian cabinet ministers, generals and intelligence officers. With his beautiful German wife, he entertained lavishly, plying his guests with liquor and listening attentively to top secret confidences. Had Lotz's true identity been known, his life would have been in instant jeopardy. German-born but an Isareli citizen, he was an agent for the Israeli secret service—to whom he sent coded messages for five years before being suddenly and brutally unmasked. What followed was a nightmare of torture and imprisonment and a trial of ten charges, each one of which carried the death sentence.

Here is the nerve-wracking, suspense-filled *true* story of a supremely courageous spy who broke every rule—and lived to tell his tale.

15109—$1.50

SMASHING THE NAZI MURDER MACHINE!

RESCUE IN DENMARK
by Harold Flender

The hated Nazis terrified the bravest of men, but when
Hitler decided to send the Jews of Denmark to the gas
chambers, the Danes rebelled and defied the German
murderers.

The Nazis gave fair warning—anyone caught giving aid
to a Jew would suffer the same fate as the Jews. Still, the
Danes would not give in, and their resistance grew. From
the King to the lowest delivery boy, Denmark fought
back. And it makes for one of the most heroic and inspir-
ing stories of World War II.

"Impossible to stop reading . . . *everyone* should read it!"
—*The London Spectator*

15128—$1.50

THE BIGGEST EXPOSE OF THE YEAR!

J. EDGAR HOOVER: The Man In His Time
by Ralph de Toledano

This is the long-awaited biography that finally tells the *inside* story of an American legend. Here, under two covers, are all the plots, schemes and secret affairs that have been suppressed for years.

Read the behind-the-scenes stories of these explosive scandals: Bobby Kennedy's involvement with Marilyn Monroe; the tap of Martin Luther King's telephone; the rumor that J. Edgar Hoover was a homosexual; Hoover's disgust over JFK's love affairs; the FBI and Dillinger; the famous movie star whom Hoover adored; *why* Marilyn Monroe killed herself; and Hoover's bitter battles with Nixon's Palace Guard.

The critically acclaimed biography of 1975! Put it on your must-read list!

17103—$1.75